I0758911

ARKANSAS PETITIONERS, ETC. 1800, 1810 [1795-1814]

(1800 begins at page 4)

(1810 begins at page 6)

Copyright 17 February 2021
Stemmons Publishing
1078 Shields Lane
South Jordan, Utah 84095

BIBLIOGRAPHY FOR ARKANSAS PETITIONERS, ETC. 1800, 1810 [1795-1814]

United States, Department of State, compiled and edited by Clarence Edwin Carter, *The Territorial Papers of the United States* Washington, D.C.: Government Printing Office, 1934-1962. 26 volumes. National Archives microfilm publications: M0721

    vol. 1. The Territorial Papers of the United States, General.
    vols. II & III The Territory Northwest of the River Ohio, 1787-1803.
    vol. IV The Territory South of the River Ohio, 1790-1796.
    vols. V & VI The Territory of Mississippi, 1798-1817.
    vols. VII & VIII The Territory of Indiana, 1800-1816.
    vol. IX The Territory of Orleans, 1803-1812.
    vols. X - XII The Territory of Michigan, 1805-1837.
    vols. XIII - XV The Territory of Louisiana-Missouri, 1803-1821.
    vols. XVI & XVII The Territory of Illinois, 1809-1818.
    vol. XVIII The Territory of Alabama, 1817-1819.
    vols. XIX - XXI The Territory of Arkansas, 1819-1836.
    vols. XXII - XXVI The Territory of Florida, 1821-1845.

[Please note: *Larger lists of names, such as petitions, etc., will be entered into the database. Names found in regular governmental/public transactions that contain no individual biographical details will not be extracted.*]

AR-01 **ARKANSAS PETITIONERS, ETC. 1800, 1810 [1795-1814]** This book compiled from *Territorial Papers of the United States* contains 261 entries and is a partial replacement for the missing federal censuses of 1800 and 1810. As a result, it is a very helpful resource in establishing residence of people in Arkansas during that early formative period in the state's history. These people include some of earliest you will find that established the foundation of what was to become the great state that Arkansas now is. This also makes it possible to determine what other records might be available for further research. Some additional biographical details may be included, and possible relationships with others may be revealed. For information on how to obtain this book search by the title at Amazon.com. This comes automatically with a paperback binding. For information on how to obtain this book search by the title or "Books by John Stemmons" at Amazon.com. This comes automatically with a paperback binding. It includes but is not limited to petitions regarding:

- Issues relating to land.
- Inhabitants of Arkansas District expressing concern about the hostile attitude of the Cherokees nearby.
- Issues about military and local officers.

INDEXES

Indexes are expensive to compile.

Which is why many books do not have them. Most that do just have a simple name index. A noteworthy exception is the *Territorial Papers of the United States* which gives some limited context as explained below.

Indexes are expensive but using modern technology we at Stemmons Publishing have included nearly all the context you may need. 100% context is probably not possible such as in a census that lists multiple neighbors. Search for entries of the same page in our book(s) or the original document if you require more information.

PUBLICATIONS FROM STEMMONS PUBLISHING

These following publications are not just traditional alphabetical lists of names, they include the context of information with each name!!

Why is that so important? Because many of the names in our books were obtained from various sources including South Carolina jury lists, the *Territorial Papers of the United States* (28 volumes each with its own index), petitions, tax lists, etc., and like most books with indexes common names require a lot of time to check each entry in the index. Can you imagine how many Smiths you would have to go through page-by-page for a compilation the size of *Territorial Papers of the United States*? Their indexes provide some context such as signing a petition. No explanation is given of what, when, or why the petition was made. Because we have included the context with each name, you can easily search all the Smiths, Taylors, Browns, Williams, etc., without all the drudgery! And since most of us have common surnames, we may need some help. Now, the originals of the South Carolina jury lists are housed in the South Carolina Department of Archives and History. Therefore, you may not have access to the originals. The way we index names means it is almost as good as being at the Archives yourself and doubly so since these documents are loose papers and do not have an original index. Our books provide an enhanced way of using *Territorial Papers of the United States* that the original compilers did not envision. So, if you have this collection, your obtaining our books compiled from those volumes will help your access to *Territorial Papers of the United States* even if you are not interested in our books about South Carolina jury lists. Now, that's what I call achieving the potential of a real index! It takes the bare skeleton of a name on a list and covers it with the flesh, hair, eyes, etc., of a human body. The names are more able to stand alone by themselves than is the case with a traditional index. We did not index subjects. *Territorial Papers of the United States* did.

Checking a name from our books and going to the page in *Territorial Papers of the United States* will show the list of names. Those listed next to the person of interest may be neighbors and relatives.

4 Names

Winters, Elisha, Spanish North America Arkansas District

Winters, Elisha, Male

Protest, 4 Oct 1819, to the President from Joshua G. Clarke of Claiborne County, Mississippi against lands granted to Elisha Winters, William Winters, and Gabl Winters by the King of Spain being surveyed for Military Bounty land [pp. 114-5].

"Joshua G. Clarke to the President

STATE OF MISSISSIPPI, CLAIBORNE COUNTY, G PORT, 4 Octo 1819

To his Excellency, the President of the U States.

A Protest.

BE IT KNOWN, That the Governor Genl of the late Province of Louisiana, when under the Dominion of the King of Spain. On the twenty seventh day of June, in the year of our lord, one thousand, seven hundred & ninety seven; did Grant, to Elisha Winters, one Million Arpents of Land, to William Winters & Gabl Winters, sons of Elisha Winters, each, two Hundred & fifty thousands Arpents, of Land; to be located, in the District of Arkansas, by the Commandant who was charged, with the location of said Concessions— And be it further Known, that Elisha Winters & William Winters, were put into the Possession of the lands, so granted; and the boundary & courses designated, & Seisin given by the Commandant, in due form; in the Spring of 1798. That Gabl Winter, being a Minor, his lands were designated.

And be it, further Known, that all the Conditions, of the Grants to Elisha Winters & William Winters, were complied with, & that the said Elisha & William Winters, by themselves & tenants & grantees have been in the actual & quiet & peaceable possessions of said lands since the Spring of the year, One thousand seven hundred & ninety eight, & which lands are now in the quiet & peaceable possession of the said Heirs & grantees of the said Elisha & William Winters. And be

[page 115] it further Known, that legal Entries, of said Lands, were made, in the Land office of the U States, at St Louis & the Title papers & other evidence, were filed, according to the provisions of the several acts of Congress, for the final adjustment of the land Titles of said Territory.

And be it further known, that said claims are now pending before the Congress of the U. States. That the H of Representatives of the U S. at their Session of 1817, did by a Select Committee, Report in favor of Confirming the titles, of Elisha & William Winters; which Report is still pending & undecided by the Congress of the U S.

And whereas it appears, that the Surveyors, under the authority of the U States, are now locating & laying off, said Lands, for Military bounty lands; thereby interfering with the rights & interests of the Undersigned, & his Co-tenants in Common.—

The undersigned, for himself & his Co-tenants in Common, in the said grants of Lands, to Elisha Winters William Winters & Gabl Winters, Solomnly protests, against the surveying or disposing of said lands, or any part thereof, by the United States, as Military bounty lands, or otherwise; until the titles of the Claimants of said lands, are decided by Congress, or some Competent tribunal according to Law.

And the Undersigned, further respectfully desires, that this Protest, may be entd as a Caveat, in the Proper Office, agt the issuing any Patent, from the U. States, for said lands; until their rights are adjudicated & determined by a Competent Tribunal.

Which Protest, is respectfully, Submitted, to the Consideration of the President of the U States by

J   G CLARKE

for himself & Co-tenants in Common." [pp. 114-5]

Territorial Papers of the US - volume: 19 page: 114

Winters, Gabl,   Spanish North America
   Arkansas District
   Winters, Gabl, Male

Protest, 4 Oct 1819, to the President from Joshua G. Clarke of Claiborne County, Mississippi against lands granted to Elisha Winters, William Winters, and Gabl Winters by the King of Spain being surveyed for Military Bounty land [pp. 114-5].

"Joshua G. Clarke to the President

STATE OF MISSISSIPPI, CLAIBORNE COUNTY, G PORT, 4 Octo 1819

To his Excellency, the President of the U States.

A Protest.

BE IT KNOWN, That the Governor Genl of the late Province of Louisiana, when under the Dominion of the King of Spain. On the twenty seventh day of June, in the year of our lord, one thousand, seven hundred & ninety seven; did Grant, to Elisha Winters, one Million Arpents of Land, to William Winters & Gabl Winters, sons of Elisha Winters, each, two Hundred & fifty thousands Arpents, of Land; to be located, in the District of Arkensas, by the Commandant who was charged, with the location of said Concessions— And be it further Known, that Elisha Winters & William Winters, were put into the Possession of the lands, so granted; and the boundary & courses designated, & Seisin given by the Commandant, in due form; in the Spring of 1798. That Gabl Winter, being a Minor, his lands were designated.

And be it, further Known, that all the Conditions, of the Grants to Elisha Winters & William Winters, were complied with, & that the said Elisha & William Winters, by themselves & tenants & grantees have been in the actual & quiet & peaceable possessions of said lands since the Spring of the year, One thousand seven hundred & ninety eight, & which lands are now in the quiet & peaceable possession of the said Heirs & grantees of the said Elisha & William Winters. And be [page 115] it further Known, that legal Entries, of said Lands, were made, in the Land office of the U States, at St Louis & the Title papers & other evidence, were filed, according to the provisions of the several acts of Congress, for the final adjustment of the land Titles of said Territory.

And be it further known, that said claims are now pending before the Congress of the U. States.

That the H of Representatives of the U S. at their Session of 1817, did by a Select Committee, Report in favor of Confirming the titles, of Elisha & William Winters; which Report is still pending & undecided by the Congress of the U S.

And whereas it appears, that the Surveyors, under the authority of the U States, are now locating & laying off, said Lands, for Military bounty lands; thereby interfering with the rights & interests of the Undersigned, & his Co-tenants in Common.—

The undersigned, for himself & his Co-tenants in Common, in the said grants of Lands, to Elisha Winters William Winters & Gabl Winters, Solomnly protests, against the surveying or disposing of said lands, or any part thereof, by the United States, as Military bounty lands, or otherwise; until the titles of the Claimants of said lands, are decided by Congress, or some Competent tribunal according to Law.

And the Undersigned, further respectfully desires, that this Protest, may be entd as a Caveat, in the Proper Office, agt the issuing any Patent, from the U. States, for said lands; until their rights are adjudicated & determined by a Competent Tribunal.

Which Protest, is respectfully, Submitted, to the Consideration of the President of the U States by

                              J   G
CLARKE
                     for himself & Co-tenants in Common." [pp. 114-5]

Territorial Papers of the US - volume: 19 page: 114

Winters, William,   Spanish North America
   Arkansas District
   Winters, William,   Male

Protest, 4 Oct 1819, to the President from Joshua G. Clarke of Claiborne County, Mississippi against lands granted to Elisha Winters, William Winters, and Gabl Winters by the King of Spain being surveyed for Military Bounty land [pp. 114-5].

"Joshua G. Clarke to the President

STATE OF MISSISSIPPI, CLAIBORNE COUNTY, G PORT, 4 Octo 1819

To his Excellency, the President of the U States.

A Protest.

BE IT KNOWN, That the Governor Genl of the late Province of Louisiana, when under the Dominion of the King of Spain. On the twenty seventh day of June, in the year of our lord, one thousand, seven hundred & ninety seven; did Grant, to Elisha Winters, one Million Arpents of Land, to William Winters & Gabl Winters, sons of Elisha Winters, each, two Hundred & fifty thousands Arpents, of Land; to be located, in the District of Arkansas, by the Commandant who was charged, with the location of said Concessions— And be it further Known, that Elisha Winters & William Winters, were put into the Possession of the lands, so granted; and the boundary & courses designated, & Seisin given by the Commandant, in due form; in the Spring of 1798. That Gabl Winter, being a Minor, his lands were designated.

And be it, further Known, that all the Conditions, of the Grants to Elisha Winters & William Winters, were complied with, & that the said Elisha & William Winters, by themselves & tenants & grantees have been in the actual & quiet & peaceable possessions of said lands since the Spring of the year, One thousand seven hundred & ninety eight, & which lands are now in the quiet & peaceable possession of the said Heirs & grantees of the said Elisha & William Winters. And be [page 115] it further Known, that legal Entries, of said Lands, were made, in the Land office of the U States, at St Louis & the Title papers & other evidence, were filed, according to the provisions of the several acts of Congress, for the final adjustment of the land Titles of said Territory.

And be it further known, that said claims are now pending before the Congress of the U. States. That the H of Representatives of the U S. at their Session of 1817, did by a Select Committee,

Report in favor of Confirming the titles, of Elisha & William Winters; which Report is still pending & undecided by the Congress of the U S.

And whereas it appears, that the Surveyors, under the authority of the U States, are now locating & laying off, said Lands, for Military bounty lands; thereby interfering with the rights & interests of the Undersigned, & his Co-tenants in Common.—

The undersigned, for himself & his Co-tenants in Common, in the said grants of Lands, to Elisha Winters William Winters & Gabl Winters, Solomnly protests, against the surveying or disposing of said lands, or any part thereof, by the United States, as Military bounty lands, or otherwise; until the titles of the Claimants of said lands, are decided by Congress, or some Competent tribunal according to Law.

And the Undersigned, further respectfully desires, that this Protest, may be entd as a Caveat, in the Proper Office, agt the issuing any Patent, from the U. States, for said lands; until their rights are adjudicated & determined by a Competent Tribunal.

Which Protest, is respectfully, Submitted, to the Consideration of the President of the U States by

J   G CLARKE

for himself & Co-tenants in Common." [pp. 114-5]
Territorial Papers of the US - volume: 19 page: 114

ARKANSAS PETITIONERS, ETC. 1810 [1805-1814]

257 Names

Alton, Richard H.,   Louisiana-Missouri Territory
Alton, Richard H.,   Male
Name on petition, 9 Sep 1811, to Congress from inhabitants of Arkansas (most depend on agriculture) stating that executive/legislative/judicial power is combined in one & 2/3 of their claims were rejected. They seek representative government [471-79].
Territorial Papers of the US - volume: 14 page: 472
Arrel, James, Louisiana-Missouri Territory
Arrel, James,   Male

Name on a petition, received 14 Apr 1812, to the Secretary of War from inhabitants of Arkansas District expressing concern about the hostile attitude of the Cherokees nearby. They ask for "two or more Companies" for protection [pages 544-45].
Territorial Papers of the US - volume: 14 page: 545

Ballard, William,   Louisiana-Missouri Territory
          Ballard, William,   Male
Name on petition, 9 Sep 1811, to Congress from inhabitants of Arkansas (most depend on agriculture) stating that executive/legislative/judicial power is combined in one & 2/3 of their claims were rejected. They seek representative government [471-79].
Territorial Papers of the US - volume: 14 page: 472

Ballard, William,   Louisiana-Missouri Territory
          Ballard, William,   Male
Name on a petition, referred 11 Mar 1812, to Congress by inhabitants of Arkansas District seeking help, stating they were unaware of the deadline for filing claims. Many had received Spanish grants 10 to 25 years previously [pages 526-29].
Territorial Papers of the US - volume: 14 page: 528

Bates, Frederick, Esquire   Louisiana-Missouri Territory
          Bates, Frederick, Esquire   Male
He is mentioned in a petition, referred 11 Mar 1812, to Congress by inhabitants of Arkansas District [pages 526-29].
". . . the Board of Commissioners, resolved to sit in the several Districts of the Territory, for the purpose of receiving the notices of Land Claims and taking evidence, relative thereto; Frederick Bates Esquire, one of said Commissioners, performed his Tour, as far down the Mississippi river, as Hopefield, opposite the Chickasaw Bluffs--his appointment, to sit at the Village of Arkansas, having, but a few days previous ["previous" is underlined] to the Time, (limited by Law for the Entry of Claims) expir'd before his arrival, in consequence of his being seized with a Fever-- nevertheless, he thought proper, by request of the Claimants to receive the Papers, Notice & other Evidence of Claims, with the belief, that Congress would make some provision for rendering those entries valid, when the situation should be known to them through the Commissioners: and, We your Petitioners further state, that the circumstances of those entries were immediately made known to the Secretary of the Treasury, by letter, from Frederic Bates Esquire [footnote: 'July 22, 1808, printed, Marshall (ed.), Bates Papers, II, 7-11. See also his statement to the land commissioners, Aug. 15, 1808, ibid., pp. 11-18.'], to which, it does not appear any answer was ever receiv'd; neither has any Law been passed by Congress for their relief;"
Territorial Papers of the US - volume: 14 page: 527

Belemont, Canroyd,   Louisiana-Missouri Territory
          Belemont, Canroyd,   Male
          "MS. faded."
Name on petition, 9 Sep 1811, to Congress from inhabitants of Arkansas (most depend on agriculture) stating that executive/legislative/judicial power is combined in one & 2/3 of their claims were rejected. They seek representative government [471-79].
Territorial Papers of the US - volume: 14 page: 472

Benet, Rafael, Louisiana-Missouri Territory
          Benet, Rafael, Male
          He signed his name with an "x".
Name on petition, 9 Sep 1811, to Congress from inhabitants of Arkansas (most depend on agriculture) stating that executive/legislative/judicial power is combined in one & 2/3 of their claims were rejected. They seek representative government [471-79].
Territorial Papers of the US - volume: 14 page: 472

Billingsley, Jno,   Louisiana-Missouri Territory   Arkansas County
          Billingsley, Jno,   Male
He is a Township Justice "For the Settlements" on a list of civil officers dated 1 Oct 1814.
Territorial Papers of the US - volume: 14 page: 795

Bloinosaw, Pere,   Louisiana-Missouri Territory
          Bloinosaw, Pere,   Male

Name on a petition, referred 11 Mar 1812, to Congress by inhabitants of Arkansas District seeking help, stating they were unaware of the deadline for filing claims. Many had received Spanish grants 10 to 25 years previously [pages 526-29].
Territorial Papers of the US - volume: 14 page: 528

Bogie, Joseph, Louisiana-Missouri Territory
    Bogie, Joseph, Male
Name on a petition, referred 11 Mar 1812, to Congress by inhabitants of Arkansas District seeking help, stating they were unaware of the deadline for filing claims. Many had received Spanish grants 10 to 25 years previously [pages 526-29].
Territorial Papers of the US - volume: 14 page: 528

Bogy, Chale,   Louisiana-Missouri Territory
    Bogy, Chale,   Male
Name on petition, 9 Sep 1811, to Congress from inhabitants of Arkansas (most depend on agriculture) stating that executive/legislative/judicial power is combined in one & 2/3 of their claims were rejected. They seek representative government [471-79].
Territorial Papers of the US - volume: 14 page: 472

Bogy, Charle, Louisiana-Missouri Territory
    Bogy, Charle,   Male
Name on a petition, referred 11 Mar 1812, to Congress by inhabitants of Arkansas District seeking help, stating they were unaware of the deadline for filing claims. Many had received Spanish grants 10 to 25 years previously [pages 526-29].
Territorial Papers of the US - volume: 14 page: 528

Bogy, Ignace, Louisiana-Missouri Territory
    Bogy, Ignace,   Male
Name on a petition, received 14 Apr 1812, to the Secretary of War from inhabitants of Arkansas District expressing concern about the hostile attitude of the Cherokees nearby. They ask for "two or more Companies" for protection [pages 544-45].
Territorial Papers of the US - volume: 14 page: 545

Bogy, Louis,   Louisiana-Missouri Territory
    Bogy, Louis,   Male

Name on petition, 9 Sep 1811, to Congress from inhabitants of Arkansas (most depend on agriculture) stating that executive/legislative/judicial power is combined in one & 2/3 of their claims were rejected. They seek representative government [471-79].
Territorial Papers of the US - volume: 14 page: 472

Bogy, Louis,   Louisiana-Missouri Territory
    Bogy, Louis,   Male
Name on a petition, referred 11 Mar 1812, to Congress by inhabitants of Arkansas District seeking help, stating they were unaware of the deadline for filing claims. Many had received Spanish grants 10 to 25 years previously [pages 526-29].
Territorial Papers of the US - volume: 14 page: 528

Bougie, Chas, Louisiana-Missouri   Territory
    Arkansas District County,,
    Bougie, Chas,   Male
He was appointed Ensign in the militia for the "District of Arkansaw", certified 8 Jul 1806.
Territorial Papers of the US - volume: 13 page: 549

Bougie, Joseph,   Louisiana-Missouri Territory   Arkansas District County,,
    Bougie, Joseph,   Male
He was appointed one of the "Justices of the peace and common Pleas" for the "District of Arkansaw", certified 8 Jul 1806.
Territorial Papers of the US - volume: 13 page: 546

Bougy, Joseph,   Louisiana-Missouri Territory
    Bougy, Joseph, Male
Name on petition, 9 Sep 1811, to Congress from inhabitants of Arkansas (most depend on agriculture) stating that executive/legislative/judicial power is combined in one & 2/3 of their claims were rejected. They seek representative government [471-79].
Territorial Papers of the US - volume: 14 page: 472

Brainbae, Wm,   Louisiana-Missouri Territory
    Brainbae, Wm, Male
    He signed his name with an "x".
Name on a petition, referred 11 Mar 1812, to Congress by inhabitants of Arkansas District

seeking help, stating they were unaware of the deadline for filing claims. Many had received Spanish grants 10 to 25 years previously [pages 526-29].
Territorial Papers of the US - volume: 14 page: 528

Brambac, W,   Louisiana-Missouri Territory
      Brambac, W,   Male
      He signed his name with an "x".
Name on petition, 9 Sep 1811, to Congress from inhabitants of Arkansas (most depend on agriculture) stating that executive/legislative/judicial power is combined in one & 2/3 of their claims were rejected. They seek representative government [471-79].
Territorial Papers of the US - volume: 14 page: 472

Bright, Jacob, Louisiana-Missouri   Territory
      Arkansas District County,,
      Bright, Jacob,   Male
He was appointed "Lt of Cavalry" in the militia for the "District of Arkansaw", certified 8 Jul 1806.
Territorial Papers of the US - volume: 13 page: 549

Bruff, James,   Louisiana-Missouri Territory
      Bruff, James,   Male
Name on a petition, referred 11 Mar 1812, to Congress by inhabitants of Arkansas District seeking help, stating they were unaware of the deadline for filing claims. Many had received Spanish grants 10 to 25 years previously [pages 526-29].
Territorial Papers of the US - volume: 14 page: 528

Bruff, James,   Louisiana-Missouri Territory
      Bruff, James,   Male
Name on petition, 9 Sep 1811, to Congress from inhabitants of Arkansas (most depend on agriculture) stating that executive/legislative/judicial power is combined in one & 2/3 of their claims were rejected. They seek representative government [471-79].
Territorial Papers of the US - volume: 14 page: 472

Budent, Alex,   Louisiana-Missouri Territory
      Budent, Alex,   Male
Name on a petition, received 14 Apr 1812, to the Secretary of War from inhabitants of Arkansas District expressing concern about the hostile attitude of the Cherokees nearby. They ask for "two or more Companies" for protection [pages 544-45].
Territorial Papers of the US - volume: 14 page: 545

Buret, Pier,   Louisiana-Missouri Territory
      Buret, Pier,   Male
      He signed his name with an "x".
Name on a petition, referred 11 Mar 1812, to Congress by inhabitants of Arkansas District seeking help, stating they were unaware of the deadline for filing claims. Many had received Spanish grants 10 to 25 years previously [pages 526-29].
Territorial Papers of the US - volume: 14 page: 528

Burrasau, Pere,   Louisiana-Missouri Territory
      Burrasau, Pere, Male
Name on a petition, received 14 Apr 1812, to the Secretary of War from inhabitants of Arkansas District expressing concern about the hostile attitude of the Cherokees nearby. They ask for "two or more Companies" for protection [pages 544-45].
Territorial Papers of the US - volume: 14 page: 545

Burrasaw, Pere,   Louisiana-Missouri Territory
      Burrasaw, Pere,   Male
Name on petition, 9 Sep 1811, to Congress from inhabitants of Arkansas (most depend on agriculture) stating that executive/legislative/judicial power is combined in one & 2/3 of their claims were rejected. They seek representative government [471-79].
Territorial Papers of the US - volume: 14 page: 472

Carnehan, John,   Louisiana-Missouri Territory   Arkansas County
      Carnehan, John,   Male
He is a Township Justice "For the Settlements" on a list of civil officers dated 1 Oct 1814.
Territorial Papers of the US - volume: 14 page: 795

Cassidy, Henry,   Louisiana-Missouri Territory   Arkansas County
      Cassidy, Henry,   Male
He is a Township Justice "For the Settlements" on a list of civil officers dated 1 Oct 1814.

Territorial Papers of the US - volume: 14 page: 795

Cassidy, Henry, Louisiana-Missouri Territory

Cassidy, Henry, Male

Name on petition, 9 Sep 1811, to Congress from inhabitants of Arkansas (most depend on agriculture) stating that executive/legislative/judicial power is combined in one & 2/3 of their claims were rejected. They seek representative government [471-79].

Territorial Papers of the US - volume: 14 page: 472

Cassidy, Henry, Louisiana-Missouri Territory

Cassidy, Henry, Male

Name on a petition, received 14 Apr 1812, to the Secretary of War from inhabitants of Arkansas District expressing concern about the hostile attitude of the Cherokees nearby. They ask for "two or more Companies" for protection [pages 544-45].

Territorial Papers of the US - volume: 14 page: 545

Cassidy, Henry, Louisiana-Missouri Territory New Madrid County

Cassidy, Henry, Male

On 1 Apr 1813, he was made a Township Justice for the "Village of Arkensas & adjt Settlements".

Territorial Papers of the US - volume: 14 page: 650

Cassidy, Henry, Louisiana-Missouri Territory

Cassidy, Henry, Male

Name on a petition, referred 11 Mar 1812, to Congress by inhabitants of Arkansas District seeking help, stating they were unaware of the deadline for filing claims. Many had received Spanish grants 10 to 25 years previously [pages 526-29].

Territorial Papers of the US - volume: 14 page: 528

Cassidy, P, Louisiana-Missouri Territory

Cassidy, P, Male

Name on petition, 9 Sep 1811, to Congress from inhabitants of Arkansas (most depend on agriculture) stating that executive/legislative/judicial power is combined in one & 2/3 of their claims were rejected. They seek representative government [471-79].

Territorial Papers of the US - volume: 14 page: 472

Cassidy, Patrick, Louisiana-Missouri Territory Arkansas County

Cassidy, Patrick, Male

He is Clerk of Arkansas County on a list of civil officers dated 1 Oct 1814.

Territorial Papers of the US - volume: 14 page: 795

Cassidy, Patrick, Louisiana-Missouri Territory

Cassidy, Patrick, Male

Name on a petition, referred 11 Mar 1812, to Congress by inhabitants of Arkansas District seeking help, stating they were unaware of the deadline for filing claims. Many had received Spanish grants 10 to 25 years previously [pages 526-29].

Territorial Papers of the US - volume: 14 page: 528

Cates, Issac, Louisiana-Missouri Territory Arkansas County

Cates, Issac, Male

He is a Township Justice "For the Settlements" on a list of civil officers dated 1 Oct 1814.

Territorial Papers of the US - volume: 14 page: 795

Chisholm, John D, Louisiana-Missouri Territory

Chisholm, John D, Male

Name on petition, 9 Sep 1811, to Congress from inhabitants of Arkansas (most depend on agriculture) stating that executive/legislative/judicial power is combined in one & 2/3 of their claims were rejected. They seek representative government [471-79].

Territorial Papers of the US - volume: 14 page: 472

Chisholm, John D., Louisiana-Missouri Territory

Chisholm, John D., Male

Name on a petition, referred 11 Mar 1812, to Congress by inhabitants of Arkansas District seeking help, stating they were unaware of the deadline for filing claims. Many had received Spanish grants 10 to 25 years previously [pages 526-29].

Territorial Papers of the US - volume: 14 page: 528

Chisolm, J G, Louisiana-Missouri Territory

Chisolm, J G,   Male
Name on petition, 9 Sep 1811, to Congress from inhabitants of Arkansas (most depend on agriculture) stating that executive/legislative/judicial power is combined in one & 2/3 of their claims were rejected. They seek representative government [471-79].
Territorial Papers of the US - volume: 14 page: 472
Chisolm, J. G.,   Louisiana-Missouri Territory
          Chisolm, J. G., Male
Name on a petition, referred 11 Mar 1812, to Congress by inhabitants of Arkansas District seeking help, stating they were unaware of the deadline for filing claims. Many had received Spanish grants 10 to 25 years previously [pages 526-29].
Territorial Papers of the US - volume: 14 page: 528
Clary, Robert, Louisiana-Missouri Territory
          Clary, Robert, Male
Name on a petition, referred 11 Mar 1812, to Congress by inhabitants of Arkansas District seeking help, stating they were unaware of the deadline for filing claims. Many had received Spanish grants 10 to 25 years previously [pages 526-29].
Territorial Papers of the US - volume: 14 page: 528
Clary, Robt,   Louisiana-Missouri Territory
          Clary, Robt,   Male
Name on petition, 9 Sep 1811, to Congress from inhabitants of Arkansas (most depend on agriculture) stating that executive/legislative/judicial power is combined in one & 2/3 of their claims were rejected. They seek representative government [471-79].
Territorial Papers of the US - volume: 14 page: 472
Cornwell, John,   Louisiana-Missouri Territory
          Cornwell, John,   Male
Name on a petition, received 14 Apr 1812, to the Secretary of War from inhabitants of Arkansas District expressing concern about the hostile attitude of the Cherokees nearby. They ask for "two or more Companies" for protection [pages 544-45].

Territorial Papers of the US - volume: 14 page: 545
Craft, James, Louisiana-Missouri Territory
          Craft, James,   Male
Name on petition, 9 Sep 1811, to Congress from inhabitants of Arkansas (most depend on agriculture) stating that executive/legislative/judicial power is combined in one & 2/3 of their claims were rejected. They seek representative government [471-79].
Territorial Papers of the US - volume: 14 page: 472
Craft, James, Louisiana-Missouri Territory
          Craft, James,   Male
Name on a petition, referred 11 Mar 1812, to Congress by inhabitants of Arkansas District seeking help, stating they were unaware of the deadline for filing claims. Many had received Spanish grants 10 to 25 years previously [pages 526-29].
Territorial Papers of the US - volume: 14 page: 528
Cramer, Christian,   Louisiana-Missouri Territory
          Cramer, Christian,   Male
Name on petition, 9 Sep 1811, to Congress from inhabitants of Arkansas (most depend on agriculture) stating that executive/legislative/judicial power is combined in one & 2/3 of their claims were rejected. They seek representative government [471-79].
Territorial Papers of the US - volume: 14 page: 472
Crook, Wm,   Louisiana-Missouri Territory
          Crook, Wm,   Male
Name on a petition, received 14 Apr 1812, to the Secretary of War from inhabitants of Arkansas District expressing concern about the hostile attitude of the Cherokees nearby. They ask for "two or more Companies" for protection [pages 544-45].
Territorial Papers of the US - volume: 14 page: 545
Currin, James,   Louisiana-Missouri Territory   Arkansas County
          Currin, James, Male
He is a Township Justice "For the Settlements" on a list of civil officers dated 1 Oct 1814.
Territorial Papers of the US - volume: 14 page: 795

Currin, Lemuel,   Louisiana-Missouri Territory   Arkansas County
                Currin, Lemuel,   Male
He is Coroner of Arkansas County on a list of civil officers dated 1 Oct 1814.
Territorial Papers of the US - volume: 14 page: 795

Daniel, Wright,   Louisiana-Missouri Territory   Arkansas County
        Daniel, Wright, Male
He is a Judge for Arkansas County on a list of civil officers dated 1 Oct 1814.
Territorial Papers of the US - volume: 14 page: 795

Darden, Joseph,   Louisiana-Missouri Territory
                Darden, Joseph,   Male
Name on petition, 9 Sep 1811, to Congress from inhabitants of Arkansas (most depend on agriculture)   stating   that executive/legislative/judicial power is combined in one & 2/3 of their claims were rejected. They seek representative government [471-79].
Territorial Papers of the US - volume: 14 page: 472

de Vaugine, Francis,   Louisiana-Missouri Territory   Arkansas County
        de Vaugine, Francis,   Male
He is a Judge for Arkansas County on a list of civil officers dated 1 Oct 1814.
Territorial Papers of the US - volume: 14 page: 795

Delauny, David,   Louisiana-Missouri Territory   Arkansas District County,,
        Delauny, David,   Male
He was appointed "Inspector and Adjutant General with the rank of Major" in the militia for the "District of Arkansaw", certified 8 Jul 1806.
Territorial Papers of the US - volume: 13 page: 549

Demont, Louis,   Louisiana-Missouri Territory
        Demont, Louis, Male
Name on a petition, received 14 Apr 1812, to the Secretary of War from inhabitants of Arkansas District expressing concern about the hostile attitude of the Cherokees nearby. They ask for "two or more Companies" for protection [pages 544-45].

Territorial Papers of the US - volume: 14 page: 545

deruseux, Joseph,   Louisiana-Missouri Territory
        deruseux, Joseph,   Male
Name on petition, 9 Sep 1811, to Congress from inhabitants of Arkansas (most depend on agriculture)   stating   that executive/legislative/judicial power is combined in one & 2/3 of their claims were rejected. They seek representative government [471-79].
Territorial Papers of the US - volume: 14 page: 472

Des Reuisseaux, Bte,   Louisiana-Missouri Territory
        Des Reuisseaux, Bte,   Male
Name on petition, 9 Sep 1811, to Congress from inhabitants of Arkansas (most depend on agriculture)   stating   that executive/legislative/judicial power is combined in one & 2/3 of their claims were rejected. They seek representative government [471-79].
Territorial Papers of the US - volume: 14 page: 472

Des Reuisseaux, Bte,   Louisiana-Missouri Territory
        Des Reuisseaux, Bte,   Male
Name on a petition, referred 11 Mar 1812, to Congress by inhabitants of Arkansas District seeking help, stating they were unaware of the deadline for filing claims. Many had received Spanish grants 10 to 25 years previously [pages 526-29].
Territorial Papers of the US - volume: 14 page: 528

Dian, John F,   Louisiana-Missouri Territory
        Dian, John F,   Male
Name on petition, 9 Sep 1811, to Congress from inhabitants of Arkansas (most depend on agriculture)   stating   that executive/legislative/judicial power is combined in one & 2/3 of their claims were rejected. They seek representative government [471-79].
Territorial Papers of the US - volume: 14 page: 472

Dirickson, Seth,   Louisiana-Missouri Territory
        Dirickson, Seth,   Male
Name on a petition, received 14 Apr 1812, to the Secretary of War from inhabitants of Arkansas

District expressing concern about the hostile attitude of the Cherokees nearby. They ask for "two or more Companies" for protection [pages 544-45].
Territorial Papers of the US - volume: 14 page: 545

Dirickson, Seth, Louisiana-Missouri Territory
Dirickson, Seth, Male
Name on petition, 9 Sep 1811, to Congress from inhabitants of Arkansas (most depend on agriculture) stating that executive/legislative/judicial power is combined in one & 2/3 of their claims were rejected. They seek representative government [471-79].
Territorial Papers of the US - volume: 14 page: 472

Dirickson, Seth, Louisiana-Missouri Territory
Dirickson, Seth, Male
Name on a petition, referred 11 Mar 1812, to Congress by inhabitants of Arkansas District seeking help, stating they were unaware of the deadline for filing claims. Many had received Spanish grants 10 to 25 years previously [pages 526-29].
Territorial Papers of the US - volume: 14 page: 528

Dodge, Jno, Louisiana-Missouri Territory
Arkansas County
Dodge, Jno, Male
On 13 Oct 1814 he was appointed "clerk of the Superior court" for Arkansas County.
Territorial Papers of the US - volume: 15 page: 42

Donoho, Morgan, Louisiana-Missouri Territory
Donoho, Morgan, Male
Name on a petition, referred 11 Mar 1812, to Congress by inhabitants of Arkansas District seeking help, stating they were unaware of the deadline for filing claims. Many had received Spanish grants 10 to 25 years previously [pages 526-29].
Territorial Papers of the US - volume: 14 page: 528

Donoho, Morgan, Louisiana-Missouri Territory
Donoho, Morgan, Male
Name on petition, 9 Sep 1811, to Congress from inhabitants of Arkansas (most depend on agriculture) stating that executive/legislative/judicial power is combined in one & 2/3 of their claims were rejected. They seek representative government [471-79].
Territorial Papers of the US - volume: 14 page: 472

Donoho, Morgan, Louisiana-Missouri Territory
Donoho, Morgan, Male
Name on a petition, received 14 Apr 1812, to the Secretary of War from inhabitants of Arkansas District expressing concern about the hostile attitude of the Cherokees nearby. They ask for "two or more Companies" for protection [pages 544-45].
Territorial Papers of the US - volume: 14 page: 545

Dumon, Louis, Louisiana-Missouri Territory
Dumon, Louis, Male
Name on petition, 9 Sep 1811, to Congress from inhabitants of Arkansas (most depend on agriculture) stating that executive/legislative/judicial power is combined in one & 2/3 of their claims were rejected. They seek representative government [471-79].
Territorial Papers of the US - volume: 14 page: 472

Dumon, Louis, Louisiana-Missouri Territory
Dumon, Louis, Male
Name on a petition, referred 11 Mar 1812, to Congress by inhabitants of Arkansas District seeking help, stating they were unaware of the deadline for filing claims. Many had received Spanish grants 10 to 25 years previously [pages 526-29].
Territorial Papers of the US - volume: 14 page: 528

Dunn, William, Louisiana-Missouri Territory
Dunn, William, Male
Name on a petition, referred 11 Mar 1812, to Congress by inhabitants of Arkansas District seeking help, stating they were unaware of the deadline for filing claims. Many had received Spanish grants 10 to 25 years previously [pages 526-29].
Territorial Papers of the US - volume: 14 page: 528

Dunn, William,   Louisiana-Missouri Territory
        Dunn, William, Male
Name on petition, 9 Sep 1811, to Congress from inhabitants of Arkansas (most depend on agriculture) stating that executive/legislative/judicial power is combined in one & 2/3 of their claims were rejected. They seek representative government [471-79].
Territorial Papers of the US - volume: 14 page: 472
Duplasy, Btes, Louisiana-Missouri Territory
        Duplasy, Btes, Male
Name on petition, 9 Sep 1811, to Congress from inhabitants of Arkansas (most depend on agriculture) stating that executive/legislative/judicial power is combined in one & 2/3 of their claims were rejected. They seek representative government [471-79].
Territorial Papers of the US - volume: 14 page: 472
Dustasy, Btst, Louisiana-Missouri Territory
        Dustasy, Btst, Male
Name on a petition, referred 11 Mar 1812, to Congress by inhabitants of Arkansas District seeking help, stating they were unaware of the deadline for filing claims. Many had received Spanish grants 10 to 25 years previously [pages 526-29].
Territorial Papers of the US - volume: 14 page: 528
ebert, Jean, Louisiana-Missouri Territory
        ebert, Jean, Male
        He signed his name with an "x".
Name on a petition, referred 11 Mar 1812, to Congress by inhabitants of Arkansas District seeking help, stating they were unaware of the deadline for filing claims. Many had received Spanish grants 10 to 25 years previously [pages 526-29].
Territorial Papers of the US - volume: 14 page: 528
ebert, Jean, Louisiana-Missouri Territory
        ebert, Jean, Male
Name on petition, 9 Sep 1811, to Congress from inhabitants of Arkansas (most depend on agriculture) stating that executive/legislative/judicial power is combined in one & 2/3 of their claims were rejected. They seek representative government [471-79].

Territorial Papers of the US - volume: 14 page: 472
Edwards, Peter,   Louisiana-Missouri Territory
        Edwards, Peter,   Male
Name on a petition, referred 11 Mar 1812, to Congress by inhabitants of Arkansas District seeking help, stating they were unaware of the deadline for filing claims. Many had received Spanish grants 10 to 25 years previously [pages 526-29].
Territorial Papers of the US - volume: 14 page: 528
Edwards, Peter,   Louisiana-Missouri Territory
        Edwards, Peter,   Male
Name on petition, 9 Sep 1811, to Congress from inhabitants of Arkansas (most depend on agriculture) stating that executive/legislative/judicial power is combined in one & 2/3 of their claims were rejected. They seek representative government [471-79].
Territorial Papers of the US - volume: 14 page: 472
Fagot*, Andrew,   Louisiana-Missouri Territory   Arkansas County
        Fagot*, Andrew,   Male
        "Asterisks on the MS."
He is a Township Justice "For the Settlements" on a list of civil officers dated 1 Oct 1814.
Territorial Papers of the US - volume: 14 page: 795
Fagot*, Andw, Louisiana-Missouri   Territory   Arkansas County
        Fagot*, Andw, Male
        "Asterisks on the MS."
He is a Township Justice "For the Settlements" on a list of civil officers dated 1 Oct 1814.
Territorial Papers of the US - volume: 14 page: 795
Fagot, Andre, Louisiana-Missouri Territory
        Fagot, Andre, Male
Name on a petition, received 14 Apr 1812, to the Secretary of War from inhabitants of Arkansas District expressing concern about the hostile attitude of the Cherokees nearby. They ask for "two or more Companies" for protection [pages 544-45].
Territorial Papers of the US - volume: 14 page: 545

Fagot, Andw, Louisiana-Missouri Territory
New Madrid County
Fagot, Andw, Male
On 1 Apr 1813, he was made a Township Justice for the "Village of Arkansas & adjt Settlements".
Territorial Papers of the US - volume: 14 page: 650

Fagot, Andw, Louisiana-Missouri Territory
Arkansas District County,,
Fagot, Andw, Male
He was appointed "Clerk of Probate and Notary Public" for the "District of Arkansaw", certified 8 Jul 1806.
Territorial Papers of the US - volume: 13 page: 546

Fontanaut, Maurice, Louisiana-Missouri Territory
Fontanaut, Maurice, Male
Name on a petition, received 14 Apr 1812, to the Secretary of War from inhabitants of Arkansas District expressing concern about the hostile attitude of the Cherokees nearby. They ask for "two or more Companies" for protection [pages 544-45].
Territorial Papers of the US - volume: 14 page: 545

Fooy, Benja, Louisiana-Missouri Territory
Arkansas County
Fooy, Benja, Male
He is a Township Justice "For the Settlements" on a list of civil officers dated 1 Oct 1814.
Territorial Papers of the US - volume: 14 page: 795

Fooy, Benja, Louisiana-Missouri Territory
New Madrid County
Fooy, Benja, Male
On 1 Apr 1813, he was made a Township Justice for the "Settlements of Hope Field & St. Francis".
Territorial Papers of the US - volume: 14 page: 650

fowler, John, Louisiana-Missouri Territory
fowler, John, Male
Name on a petition, referred 11 Mar 1812, to Congress by inhabitants of Arkansas District seeking help, stating they were unaware of the deadline for filing claims. Many had received Spanish grants 10 to 25 years previously [pages 526-29].
Territorial Papers of the US - volume: 14 page: 528

fowler, John, Louisiana-Missouri Territory
fowler, John, Male
Name on petition, 9 Sep 1811, to Congress from inhabitants of Arkansas (most depend on agriculture) stating that executive/legislative/judicial power is combined in one & 2/3 of their claims were rejected. They seek representative government [471-79].
Territorial Papers of the US - volume: 14 page: 472

Fowler, John, Louisiana-Missouri Territory
Fowler, John, Male
Name on a petition, received 14 Apr 1812, to the Secretary of War from inhabitants of Arkansas District expressing concern about the hostile attitude of the Cherokees nearby. They ask for "two or more Companies" for protection [pages 544-45].
Territorial Papers of the US - volume: 14 page: 545

Fowler, Saml, Louisiana-Missouri Territory
Fowler, Saml, Male
Name on a petition, referred 11 Mar 1812, to Congress by inhabitants of Arkansas District seeking help, stating they were unaware of the deadline for filing claims. Many had received Spanish grants 10 to 25 years previously [pages 526-29].
Territorial Papers of the US - volume: 14 page: 528

Fowler, Saml, Louisiana-Missouri Territory
Fowler, Saml, Male
Name on petition, 9 Sep 1811, to Congress from inhabitants of Arkansas (most depend on agriculture) stating that executive/legislative/judicial power is combined in one & 2/3 of their claims were rejected. They seek representative government [471-79].
Territorial Papers of the US - volume: 14 page: 472

Gates, Saml, Louisiana-Missouri Territory
Arkansas County
Gates, Saml, Male
He is a Township Justice "For the Settlements" on a list of civil officers dated 1 Oct 1814.
Territorial Papers of the US - volume: 14 page: 795

Ginet, Rafael, Louisiana-Missouri Territory
Ginet, Rafael, Male
He signed his name with an "x".

Name on a petition, referred 11 Mar 1812, to Congress by inhabitants of Arkansas District seeking help, stating they were unaware of the deadline for filing claims. Many had received Spanish grants 10 to 25 years previously [pages 526-29].
Territorial Papers of the US - volume: 14 page: 528

Goodwin, W M,   Louisiana-Missouri Territory
          Goodwin, W M,   Male
Name on petition, 9 Sep 1811, to Congress from inhabitants of Arkansas (most depend on agriculture) stating that executive/legislative/judicial power is combined in one & 2/3 of their claims were rejected. They seek representative government [471-79].
Territorial Papers of the US - volume: 14 page: 472

Goodwin, W M,   Louisiana-Missouri Territory
          Goodwin, W M,   Male
Name on a petition, received 14 Apr 1812, to the Secretary of War from inhabitants of Arkansas District expressing concern about the hostile attitude of the Cherokees nearby. They ask for "two or more Companies" for protection [pages 544-45].
Territorial Papers of the US - volume: 14 page: 545

Goodwin, W. M.,   Louisiana-Missouri Territory
          Goodwin, W. M.,   Male
Name on a petition, referred 11 Mar 1812, to Congress by inhabitants of Arkansas District seeking help, stating they were unaware of the deadline for filing claims. Many had received Spanish grants 10 to 25 years previously [pages 526-29].
Territorial Papers of the US - volume: 14 page: 528

Gore, Robert A,   Louisiana-Missouri Territory
          Gore, Robert A,   Male
Name on a petition, received 14 Apr 1812, to the Secretary of War from inhabitants of Arkansas District expressing concern about the hostile attitude of the Cherokees nearby. They ask for "two or more Companies" for protection [pages 544-45].

Territorial Papers of the US - volume: 14 page: 545

grener, Francois,   Louisiana-Missouri Territory
          grener, Francois,   Male
          He signed his name with an "x".
Name on a petition, referred 11 Mar 1812, to Congress by inhabitants of Arkansas District seeking help, stating they were unaware of the deadline for filing claims. Many had received Spanish grants 10 to 25 years previously [pages 526-29].
Territorial Papers of the US - volume: 14 page: 528

grever, Bte,   Louisiana-Missouri Territory
          grever, Bte,   Male
          He signed his name with an "x".
Name on petition, 9 Sep 1811, to Congress from inhabitants of Arkansas (most depend on agriculture) stating that executive/legislative/judicial power is combined in one & 2/3 of their claims were rejected. They seek representative government [471-79].
Territorial Papers of the US - volume: 14 page: 472

grever, Francois,   Louisiana-Missouri Territory
          grever, Francois,   Male
          He signed his name with an "x".
Name on petition, 9 Sep 1811, to Congress from inhabitants of Arkansas (most depend on agriculture) stating that executive/legislative/judicial power is combined in one & 2/3 of their claims were rejected. They seek representative government [471-79].
Territorial Papers of the US - volume: 14 page: 472

Hadin, A,   Louisiana-Missouri Territory
          Hadin, A,   Male
Name on a petition, received 14 Apr 1812, to the Secretary of War from inhabitants of Arkansas District expressing concern about the hostile attitude of the Cherokees nearby. They ask for "two or more Companies" for protection [pages 544-45].
Territorial Papers of the US - volume: 14 page: 545

Hagan, Hugh, Louisiana-Missouri Territory
          Hagan, Hugh,   Male

Name on a petition, referred 11 Mar 1812, to Congress by inhabitants of Arkansas District seeking help, stating they were unaware of the deadline for filing claims. Many had received Spanish grants 10 to 25 years previously [pages 526-29].
Territorial Papers of the US - volume: 14 page: 528

Hendry, John, Louisiana-Missouri Territory
        Hendry, John,   Male
Name on a petition, received 14 Apr 1812, to the Secretary of War from inhabitants of Arkansas District expressing concern about the hostile attitude of the Cherokees nearby. They ask for "two or more Companies" for protection [pages 544-45].
Territorial Papers of the US - volume: 14 page: 545

Hendry, John, Louisiana-Missouri Territory
        Hendry, John,   Male
Name on a petition, referred 11 Mar 1812, to Congress by inhabitants of Arkansas District seeking help, stating they were unaware of the deadline for filing claims. Many had received Spanish grants 10 to 25 years previously [pages 526-29].
Territorial Papers of the US - volume: 14 page: 528

Hendry, John, Louisiana-Missouri Territory
        Hendry, John,   Male
Name on petition, 9 Sep 1811, to Congress from inhabitants of Arkansas (most depend on agriculture) stating that executive/legislative/judicial power is combined in one & 2/3 of their claims were rejected. They seek representative government [471-79].
Territorial Papers of the US - volume: 14 page: 472

Higgins, Wm, Louisiana-Missouri Territory
        Higgins, Wm,   Male
Name on a petition, received 14 Apr 1812, to the Secretary of War from inhabitants of Arkansas District expressing concern about the hostile attitude of the Cherokees nearby. They ask for "two or more Companies" for protection [pages 544-45].
Territorial Papers of the US - volume: 14 page: 545

Horner, Will. B. R.,   Louisiana-Missouri Territory

Horner, Will. B. R.,   Male
Name on a petition, referred 11 Mar 1812, to Congress by inhabitants of Arkansas District seeking help, stating they were unaware of the deadline for filing claims. Many had received Spanish grants 10 to 25 years previously [pages 526-29].
Territorial Papers of the US - volume: 14 page: 528

Hornor, Will B. R.,   Louisiana-Missouri Territory
        Hornor, Will B. R.,   Male
Name on petition, 9 Sep 1811, to Congress from inhabitants of Arkansas (most depend on agriculture) stating that executive/legislative/judicial power is combined in one & 2/3 of their claims were rejected. They seek representative government [471-79].
Territorial Papers of the US - volume: 14 page: 472

Isaacs, Jesse, Louisiana-Missouri Territory
        Isaacs, Jesse,   Male
Name on petition, 9 Sep 1811, to Congress from inhabitants of Arkansas (most depend on agriculture) stating that executive/legislative/judicial power is combined in one & 2/3 of their claims were rejected. They seek representative government [471-79].
Territorial Papers of the US - volume: 14 page: 472

Isaacs, Jesse, Louisiana-Missouri Territory
        Isaacs, Jesse,   Male
Name on a petition, referred 11 Mar 1812, to Congress by inhabitants of Arkansas District seeking help, stating they were unaware of the deadline for filing claims. Many had received Spanish grants 10 to 25 years previously [pages 526-29].
Territorial Papers of the US - volume: 14 page: 528

Jandron, Alexi,   Louisiana-Missouri Territory
        Jandron, Alexi, Male
        He signed his name with an "x".
Name on petition, 9 Sep 1811, to Congress from inhabitants of Arkansas (most depend on agriculture) stating that executive/legislative/judicial power is combined in one & 2/3 of their claims were rejected. They seek representative government [471-79].

Territorial Papers of the US - volume: 14 page: 472

Jennings, Simeon,   Louisiana-Missouri Territory
        Jennings, Simeon,   Male
Name on a petition, received 14 Apr 1812, to the Secretary of War from inhabitants of Arkansas District expressing concern about the hostile attitude of the Cherokees nearby. They ask for "two or more Companies" for protection [pages 544-45].
Territorial Papers of the US - volume: 14 page: 545

Jennings, Simeon,   Louisiana-Missouri Territory
        Jennings, Simeon,   Male
Name on petition, 9 Sep 1811, to Congress from inhabitants of Arkansas (most depend on agriculture) stating that executive/legislative/judicial power is combined in one & 2/3 of their claims were rejected. They seek representative government [471-79].
Territorial Papers of the US - volume: 14 page: 472

Jens, Simeon, Louisiana-Missouri Territory
        Jens, Simeon,   Male
Name on a petition, referred 11 Mar 1812, to Congress by inhabitants of Arkansas District seeking help, stating they were unaware of the deadline for filing claims. Many had received Spanish grants 10 to 25 years previously [pages 526-29].
Territorial Papers of the US - volume: 14 page: 528

King, Jno,   Louisiana-Missouri   Territory
        Arkansas County
        King, Jno,   Male
He is a Township Justice "For the Settlements" on a list of civil officers dated 1 Oct 1814.
Territorial Papers of the US - volume: 14 page: 795

King, Jno,   Louisiana-Missouri   Territory
        New Madrid County
        King, Jno,   Male
On 1 Apr 1813, he was made a Township Justice for the "Upper Settts Arkansas".
Territorial Papers of the US - volume: 14 page: 650

La Meaux, Pierre,   Louisiana-Missouri Territory

La Meaux, Pierre,   Male
Name on a petition, received 14 Apr 1812, to the Secretary of War from inhabitants of Arkansas District expressing concern about the hostile attitude of the Cherokees nearby. They ask for "two or more Companies" for protection [pages 544-45].
Territorial Papers of the US - volume: 14 page: 545

la Vergne, Pierre,   Louisiana-Missouri Territory
        la Vergne, Pierre,   Male
        He signed his name with an "x".
Name on a petition, received 14 Apr 1812, to the Secretary of War from inhabitants of Arkansas District expressing concern about the hostile attitude of the Cherokees nearby. They ask for "two or more Companies" for protection [pages 544-45].
Territorial Papers of the US - volume: 14 page: 545

Ladeceur, Battist,   Louisiana-Missouri Territory
        Ladeceur, Battist,   Male
Name on a petition, received 14 Apr 1812, to the Secretary of War from inhabitants of Arkansas District expressing concern about the hostile attitude of the Cherokees nearby. They ask for "two or more Companies" for protection [pages 544-45].
Territorial Papers of the US - volume: 14 page: 545

Lafevre, Pero, Louisiana-Missouri Territory
        Lafevre, Pero,   Male
Name on a petition, received 14 Apr 1812, to the Secretary of War from inhabitants of Arkansas District expressing concern about the hostile attitude of the Cherokees nearby. They ask for "two or more Companies" for protection [pages 544-45].
Territorial Papers of the US - volume: 14 page: 545

Larkey, John, Louisiana-Missouri Territory
        Larkey, John,   Male
Name on petition, 9 Sep 1811, to Congress from inhabitants of Arkansas (most depend on agriculture) stating that executive/legislative/judicial power is combined in one & 2/3 of their claims were rejected. They seek representative government [471-79].

Territorial Papers of the US - volume: 14 page: 472

Larose, Francois,   Louisiana-Missouri Territory
        Larose, Francois,   Male
Name on a petition, received 14 Apr 1812, to the Secretary of War from inhabitants of Arkansas District expressing concern about the hostile attitude of the Cherokees nearby. They ask for "two or more Companies" for protection [pages 544-45].
Territorial Papers of the US - volume: 14 page: 545

Le fevre, Piere, fils   Louisiana-Missouri Territory
        Le fevre, Piere, fils   Male
Name on a petition, received 14 Apr 1812, to the Secretary of War from inhabitants of Arkansas District expressing concern about the hostile attitude of the Cherokees nearby. They ask for "two or more Companies" for protection [pages 544-45].
Territorial Papers of the US - volume: 14 page: 545

Lefevre, Pierre, fils   Louisiana-Missouri Territory
        Lefevre, Pierre, fils   Male
Name on a petition, referred 11 Mar 1812, to Congress by inhabitants of Arkansas District seeking help, stating they were unaware of the deadline for filing claims. Many had received Spanish grants 10 to 25 years previously [pages 526-29].
Territorial Papers of the US - volume: 14 page: 528

LeFevre, Pierre, fils   Louisiana-Missouri Territory
        LeFevre, Pierre, fils   Male
Name on petition, 9 Sep 1811, to Congress from inhabitants of Arkansas (most depend on agriculture) stating that executive/legislative/judicial power is combined in one & 2/3 of their claims were rejected. They seek representative government [471-79].
Territorial Papers of the US - volume: 14 page: 472

Lefevre, Pre, Louisiana-Missouri   Territory
        Arkansas District County,,
        Lefevre, Pre,   Male

He was appointed Cornet in the militia for the "District of Arkansaw", certified 8 Jul 1806.
Territorial Papers of the US - volume: 13 page: 549

Lemon, James,   Louisiana-Missouri Territory
        Lemon, James, Male
Name on a petition, received 14 Apr 1812, to the Secretary of War from inhabitants of Arkansas District expressing concern about the hostile attitude of the Cherokees nearby. They ask for "two or more Companies" for protection [pages 544-45].
Territorial Papers of the US - volume: 14 page: 545

Lemon, John, Louisiana-Missouri Territory
        Lemon, John,   Male
Name on a petition, received 14 Apr 1812, to the Secretary of War from inhabitants of Arkansas District expressing concern about the hostile attitude of the Cherokees nearby. They ask for "two or more Companies" for protection [pages 544-45].
Territorial Papers of the US - volume: 14 page: 545

Lemon, Samuel,   Louisiana-Missouri Territory
        Lemon, Samuel,   Male
Name on petition, 9 Sep 1811, to Congress from inhabitants of Arkansas (most depend on agriculture)   stating   that executive/legislative/judicial power is combined in one & 2/3 of their claims were rejected. They seek representative government [471-79].
Territorial Papers of the US - volume: 14 page: 472

Lemon, Samuel,   Louisiana-Missouri Territory
        Lemon, Samuel,   Male
Name on a petition, referred 11 Mar 1812, to Congress by inhabitants of Arkansas District seeking help, stating they were unaware of the deadline for filing claims. Many had received Spanish grants 10 to 25 years previously [pages 526-29].
Territorial Papers of the US - volume: 14 page: 528

Lenis, R. P., Louisiana-Missouri Territory
        Lenis, R. P.,   Male

Name on a petition, referred 11 Mar 1812, to Congress by inhabitants of Arkansas District seeking help, stating they were unaware of the deadline for filing claims. Many had received Spanish grants 10 to 25 years previously [pages 526-29].
Territorial Papers of the US - volume: 14 page: 528

Lewis, Eli J,   Louisiana-Missouri Territory
Lewis, Eli J,   Male
Name on petition, 9 Sep 1811, to Congress from inhabitants of Arkansas (most depend on agriculture) stating that executive/legislative/judicial power is combined in one & 2/3 of their claims were rejected. They seek representative government [471-79].
Territorial Papers of the US - volume: 14 page: 472

Loudion, Elexis,   Louisiana-Missouri Territory
Loudion, Elexis,   Male
Name on a petition, received 14 Apr 1812, to the Secretary of War from inhabitants of Arkansas District expressing concern about the hostile attitude of the Cherokees nearby. They ask for "two or more Companies" for protection [pages 544-45].
Territorial Papers of the US - volume: 14 page: 545

Mason, Joseph,   Louisiana-Missouri Territory   Arkansas District County,,
Mason, Joseph, Male
He was appointed Sheriff for the "District of Arkansaw", certified 8 Jul 1806.
Territorial Papers of the US - volume: 13 page: 546

McCartney, John,   Louisiana-Missouri Territory
McCartney, John,   Male
Name on a petition, referred 11 Mar 1812, to Congress by inhabitants of Arkansas District seeking help, stating they were unaware of the deadline for filing claims. Many had received Spanish grants 10 to 25 years previously [pages 526-29].
Territorial Papers of the US - volume: 14 page: 528

McCartney, John,   Louisiana-Missouri Territory
McCartney, John,   Male

Name on petition, 9 Sep 1811, to Congress from inhabitants of Arkansas (most depend on agriculture) stating that executive/legislative/judicial power is combined in one & 2/3 of their claims were rejected. They seek representative government [471-79].
Territorial Papers of the US - volume: 14 page: 472

McIllmurray, Jno,   Louisiana-Missouri Territory   New Madrid County
McIllmurray, Jno,   Male
On 1 Apr 1813, he was made a Township Justice for the "Upper Settts Arkensas".
Territorial Papers of the US - volume: 14 page: 650

McIllmurray, Jno,   Louisiana-Missouri Territory   Arkansas County
McIllmurray, Jno,   Male
He is a Township Justice "For the Settlements" on a list of civil officers dated 1 Oct 1814.
Territorial Papers of the US - volume: 14 page: 795

McManis, Patrick,   Louisiana-Missouri Territory
McManis, Patrick,   Male
On the 18 Dec 1814 he was issued a "License to trade with the Indians in amety with the United States, on the river Arkansas & White River--for one
Territorial Papers of the US - volume: 15 page: 42

Menard, Jean Baptist, Louisiana-Missouri Territory
Menard, Jean Baptist,   Male
Name on a petition, referred 11 Mar 1812, to Congress by inhabitants of Arkansas District seeking help, stating they were unaware of the deadline for filing claims. Many had received Spanish grants 10 to 25 years previously [pages 526-29].
Territorial Papers of the US - volume: 14 page: 528

Menard, Js Bte,   Louisiana-Missouri Territory
Menard, Js Bte, Male
Name on petition, 9 Sep 1811, to Congress from inhabitants of Arkansas (most depend on agriculture) stating that executive/legislative/judicial power is combined in one & 2/3 of their claims were rejected. They seek representative government [471-79].

Territorial Papers of the US - volume: 14 page: 472

Metrose, Richard H., Louisiana-Missouri Territory

      Metrose, Richard H., Male

Name on a petition, referred 11 Mar 1812, to Congress by inhabitants of Arkansas District seeking help, stating they were unaware of the deadline for filing claims. Many had received Spanish grants 10 to 25 years previously [pages 526-29].

Territorial Papers of the US - volume: 14 page: 528

Miller, John, Louisiana-Missouri Territory

      Miller, John, Male

Name on a petition, referred 11 Mar 1812, to Congress by inhabitants of Arkansas District seeking help, stating they were unaware of the deadline for filing claims. Many had received Spanish grants 10 to 25 years previously [pages 526-29].

Territorial Papers of the US - volume: 14 page: 528

Miller, John, Louisiana-Missouri Territory

      Miller, John, Male

Name on petition, 9 Sep 1811, to Congress from inhabitants of Arkansas (most depend on agriculture) stating that executive/legislative/judicial power is combined in one & 2/3 of their claims were rejected. They seek representative government [471-79].

Territorial Papers of the US - volume: 14 page: 472

Miller, John, Louisiana-Missouri Territory

      Miller, John, Male

Name on petition, 9 Sep 1811, to Congress from inhabitants of Arkansas (most depend on agriculture) stating that executive/legislative/judicial power is combined in one & 2/3 of their claims were rejected. They seek representative government [471-79].

Territorial Papers of the US - volume: 14 page: 472

Miller, John, Louisiana-Missouri Territory

      Miller, John, Male

Name on a petition, received 14 Apr 1812, to the Secretary of War from inhabitants of Arkansas District expressing concern about the hostile attitude of the Cherokees nearby. They ask for "two or more Companies" for protection [pages 544-45].

Territorial Papers of the US - volume: 14 page: 545

Miller, Saml, Louisiana-Missouri Territory

      Arkansas County

      Miller, Saml, Male

He is a Township Justice "For the Settlements" on a list of civil officers dated 1 Oct 1814.

Territorial Papers of the US - volume: 14 page: 795

Milton, Richard H, Louisiana-Missouri Territory

      Milton, Richard H, Male

Name on a petition, received 14 Apr 1812, to the Secretary of War from inhabitants of Arkansas District expressing concern about the hostile attitude of the Cherokees nearby. They ask for "two or more Companies" for protection [pages 544-45].

Territorial Papers of the US - volume: 14 page: 545

Mitchell, Francis, Louisiana-Missouri Territory

      Mitchell, Francis, Male

      He signed his name with an "x".

Name on a petition, received 14 Apr 1812, to the Secretary of War from inhabitants of Arkansas District expressing concern about the hostile attitude of the Cherokees nearby. They ask for "two or more Companies" for protection [pages 544-45].

Territorial Papers of the US - volume: 14 page: 545

Mooney, D, Louisiana-Missouri Territory

      Mooney, D, Male

Name on a petition, received 14 Apr 1812, to the Secretary of War from inhabitants of Arkansas District expressing concern about the hostile attitude of the Cherokees nearby. They ask for "two or more Companies" for protection [pages 544-45].

Territorial Papers of the US - volume: 14 page: 545

Mooney, D., Louisiana-Missouri Territory

      Mooney, D., Male

Name on a petition, referred 11 Mar 1812, to Congress by inhabitants of Arkansas District seeking help, stating they were unaware of the deadline for filing claims. Many had received

Spanish grants 10 to 25 years previously [pages 526-29].
Territorial Papers of the US - volume: 14 page: 528

Mooney, D:,   Louisiana-Missouri Territory
Mooney, D:,   Male
Name on petition, 9 Sep 1811, to Congress from inhabitants of Arkansas (most depend on agriculture) stating that executive/legislative/judicial power is combined in one & 2/3 of their claims were rejected. They seek representative government [471-79].
Territorial Papers of the US - volume: 14 page: 472

Mooney, Daniel,   Louisiana-Missouri Territory   Arkansas County
Mooney, Daniel,   Male
He is Sheriff of Arkansas County on a list of civil officers dated 1 Oct 1814.
Territorial Papers of the US - volume: 14 page: 795

Moore, Amos, Louisiana-Missouri Territory
Moore, Amos, Male
Name on petition, 9 Sep 1811, to Congress from inhabitants of Arkansas (most depend on agriculture) stating that executive/legislative/judicial power is combined in one & 2/3 of their claims were rejected. They seek representative government [471-79].
Territorial Papers of the US - volume: 14 page: 472

Moore, James, Louisiana-Missouri Territory
Moore, James, Male
Name on a petition, referred 11 Mar 1812, to Congress by inhabitants of Arkansas District seeking help, stating they were unaware of the deadline for filing claims. Many had received Spanish grants 10 to 25 years previously [pages 526-29].
Territorial Papers of the US - volume: 14 page: 528

Moseley, Samuel,   Louisiana-Missouri Territory
Moseley, Samuel,   Male
Name on a petition, received 14 Apr 1812, to the Secretary of War from inhabitants of Arkansas District expressing concern about the hostile attitude of the Cherokees nearby. They ask for "two or more Companies" for protection [pages 544-45].

Territorial Papers of the US - volume: 14 page: 545

Moseley, Samuel,   Louisiana-Missouri Territory
Moseley, Samuel,   Male
Name on petition, 9 Sep 1811, to Congress from inhabitants of Arkansas (most depend on agriculture) stating that executive/legislative/judicial power is combined in one & 2/3 of their claims were rejected. They seek representative government [471-79].
Territorial Papers of the US - volume: 14 page: 472

Nixon, Robert R.,   Louisiana-Missouri Territory   New Madrid County
Nixon, Robert R.,   Male
On 1 Apr 1813, he was made a Township Justice for the "Settlements of Hope Field & St. Francis".
Territorial Papers of the US - volume: 14 page: 650

Nixon, Robert R.,   Louisiana-Missouri Territory   Arkansas County
Nixon, Robert R.,   Male
He is a Township Justice "For the Settlements" on a list of civil officers dated 1 Oct 1814.
Territorial Papers of the US - volume: 14 page: 795

Notrebe, Frederic,   Louisiana-Missouri Territory
Notrebe, Frederic,   Male
Name on a petition, received 14 Apr 1812, to the Secretary of War from inhabitants of Arkansas District expressing concern about the hostile attitude of the Cherokees nearby. They ask for "two or more Companies" for protection [pages 544-45].
Territorial Papers of the US - volume: 14 page: 545

Notrebee, Fred,   Louisiana-Missouri Territory   Arkansas County
Notrebee, Fred, Male
He is a Township Justice "For the Settlements" on a list of civil officers dated 1 Oct 1814.
Territorial Papers of the US - volume: 14 page: 795

Parker, John, Louisiana-Missouri Territory
Parker, John,   Male
Name on a petition, referred 11 Mar 1812, to Congress by inhabitants of Arkansas District seeking help, stating they were unaware of the

deadline for filing claims. Many had received Spanish grants 10 to 25 years previously [pages 526-29].

Territorial Papers of the US - volume: 14 page: 528

Parker, John, Louisiana-Missouri Territory
        Parker, John,   Male
Name on petition, 9 Sep 1811, to Congress from inhabitants of Arkansas (most depend on agriculture) stating that executive/legislative/judicial power is combined in one & 2/3 of their claims were rejected. They seek representative government [471-79].

Territorial Papers of the US - volume: 14 page: 472

Parker, Tudor,   Louisiana-Missouri Territory
        Parker, Tudor, Male
Name on a petition, received 14 Apr 1812, to the Secretary of War from inhabitants of Arkansas District expressing concern about the hostile attitude of the Cherokees nearby. They ask for "two or more Companies" for protection [pages 544-45].

Territorial Papers of the US - volume: 14 page: 545

Partville, Peter,   Louisiana-Missouri Territory
        Partville, Peter, Male
        He signed his name with an "x".
Name on a petition, referred 11 Mar 1812, to Congress by inhabitants of Arkansas District seeking help, stating they were unaware of the deadline for filing claims. Many had received Spanish grants 10 to 25 years previously [pages 526-29].

Territorial Papers of the US - volume: 14 page: 528

pertius, alexandre,   Louisiana-Missouri Territory
        pertius, alexandre,   Male
Name on a petition, received 14 Apr 1812, to the Secretary of War from inhabitants of Arkansas District expressing concern about the hostile attitude of the Cherokees nearby. They ask for "two or more Companies" for protection [pages 544-45].

Territorial Papers of the US - volume: 14 page: 545

pertuit, Pier,   Louisiana-Missouri Territory
        pertuit, Pier,   Male
        He signed his name with an "x".
Name on a petition, referred 11 Mar 1812, to Congress by inhabitants of Arkansas District seeking help, stating they were unaware of the deadline for filing claims. Many had received Spanish grants 10 to 25 years previously [pages 526-29].

Territorial Papers of the US - volume: 14 page: 528

pertuit, pier,   Louisiana-Missouri Territory
        pertuit, pier,   Male
        He signed his name with an "x".
Name on petition, 9 Sep 1811, to Congress from inhabitants of Arkansas (most depend on agriculture) stating that executive/legislative/judicial power is combined in one & 2/3 of their claims were rejected. They seek representative government [471-79].

Territorial Papers of the US - volume: 14 page: 472

peterson, Micha,   Louisiana-Missouri Territory
        peterson, Micha,   Male
Name on a petition, referred 11 Mar 1812, to Congress by inhabitants of Arkansas District seeking help, stating they were unaware of the deadline for filing claims. Many had received Spanish grants 10 to 25 years previously [pages 526-29].

Territorial Papers of the US - volume: 14 page: 528

Petterson, Michael,   Louisiana-Missouri Territory
        Petterson, Michael,   Male
Name on petition, 9 Sep 1811, to Congress from inhabitants of Arkansas (most depend on agriculture) stating that executive/legislative/judicial power is combined in one & 2/3 of their claims were rejected. They seek representative government [471-79].

Territorial Papers of the US - volume: 14 page: 472

Philips, Zach, Louisiana-Missouri   Territory
        Arkansas County
        Philips, Zach,   Male
He is a Township Justice "For the Settlements" on a list of civil officers dated 1 Oct 1814.

Territorial Papers of the US - volume: 14 page: 795

Phillip, Zauheus,   Louisiana-Missouri Territory
        Phillip, Zauheus,   Male
Name on a petition, referred 11 Mar 1812, to Congress by inhabitants of Arkansas District seeking help, stating they were unaware of the deadline for filing claims. Many had received Spanish grants 10 to 25 years previously [pages 526-29].
Territorial Papers of the US - volume: 14 page: 528
Phillips, Sylvanus,   Louisiana-Missouri Territory
        Phillips, Sylvanus,   Male
Name on a petition, referred 11 Mar 1812, to Congress by inhabitants of Arkansas District seeking help, stating they were unaware of the deadline for filing claims. Many had received Spanish grants 10 to 25 years previously [pages 526-29].
Territorial Papers of the US - volume: 14 page: 528
Phillips, Sylvanus,   Louisiana-Missouri Territory
        Phillips, Sylvanus,   Male
Name on petition, 9 Sep 1811, to Congress from inhabitants of Arkansas (most depend on agriculture)   stating   that executive/legislative/judicial power is combined in one & 2/3 of their claims were rejected. They seek representative government [471-79].
Territorial Papers of the US - volume: 14 page: 472
Phillips, Zaccheus,   Louisiana-Missouri Territory
        Phillips, Zaccheus,   Male
Name on petition, 9 Sep 1811, to Congress from inhabitants of Arkansas (most depend on agriculture)   stating   that executive/legislative/judicial power is combined in one & 2/3 of their claims were rejected. They seek representative government [471-79].
Territorial Papers of the US - volume: 14 page: 472
Pierre, Elixr,   Louisiana-Missouri Territory
        Pierre, Elixr,   Male
        He signed his name with an "x".
Name on petition, 9 Sep 1811, to Congress from inhabitants of Arkansas (most depend on agriculture)   stating   that executive/legislative/judicial power is combined in one & 2/3 of their claims were rejected. They seek representative government [471-79].
Territorial Papers of the US - volume: 14 page: 472
Pinau, Augustin,   Louisiana-Missouri Territory
        Pinau, Augustin,   Male
Name on a petition, received 14 Apr 1812, to the Secretary of War from inhabitants of Arkansas District expressing concern about the hostile attitude of the Cherokees nearby. They ask for "two or more Companies" for protection [pages 544-45].
Territorial Papers of the US - volume: 14 page: 545
Pinau, Piere,   Louisiana-Missouri Territory
        Pinau, Piere,   Male
Name on a petition, received 14 Apr 1812, to the Secretary of War from inhabitants of Arkansas District expressing concern about the hostile attitude of the Cherokees nearby. They ask for "two or more Companies" for protection [pages 544-45].
Territorial Papers of the US - volume: 14 page: 545
plassie, Louis,   Louisiana-Missouri Territory
        plassie, Louis,   Male
Name on petition, 9 Sep 1811, to Congress from inhabitants of Arkansas (most depend on agriculture)   stating   that executive/legislative/judicial power is combined in one & 2/3 of their claims were rejected. They seek representative government [471-79].
Territorial Papers of the US - volume: 14 page: 472
Plonce, Louis,   Louisiana-Missouri Territory
        Plonce, Louis,   Male
Name on a petition, referred 11 Mar 1812, to Congress by inhabitants of Arkansas District seeking help, stating they were unaware of the deadline for filing claims. Many had received Spanish grants 10 to 25 years previously [pages 526-29].
Territorial Papers of the US - volume: 14 page: 528
Pringle, Christian,   Louisiana-Missouri Territory   Arkansas District County,,
        Pringle, Christian,   Male

He was appointed Coroner for the "District of Arkansaw", certified 8 Jul 1806.
Territorial Papers of the US - volume: 13 page: 546

Racine, Tenasse,   Louisiana-Missouri Territory
        Racine, Tenasse,   Male
Name on a petition, received 14 Apr 1812, to the Secretary of War from inhabitants of Arkansas District expressing concern about the hostile attitude of the Cherokees nearby. They ask for "two or more Companies" for protection [pages 544-45].
Territorial Papers of the US - volume: 14 page: 545

Rector, ,   Louisiana-Missouri Territory
        Rector, ,   Male
He is mentioned in a petition, received 14 Apr 1812, to the Secretary of War from inhabitants of Arkansas District expressing concern about the hostile
attitude of the Cherokees nearby. They ask for "two or more Companies" for protection [pages 544-45].
"A Party of Cherokees Indians living on the River St Francois within the Jurisdiction of this Destrict [Arkansas]; . . . that two of said Cherokees have lately
 murdered A man by the name of [blank] Rector near their settlement on said River, they met him on the road murdered him, Cut open his body, tore out
his bowels and afterwards cut and mangled his body in the most savage manner."
Territorial Papers of the US - volume: 14 page: 544

Refeld, Charles,   Louisiana-Missouri Territory
        Refeld, Charles,   Male
Name on petition, 9 Sep 1811, to Congress from inhabitants of Arkansas (most depend on agriculture) stating that executive/legislative/judicial power is combined in one & 2/3 of their claims were rejected. They seek representative government [471-79].
Territorial Papers of the US - volume: 14 page: 472

Refeldt, Charles,   Louisiana-Missouri Territory   Arkansas District County,,
        Refeldt, Charles,   Male

He was appointed one of the "Justices of the peace and common Pleas" for the "District of Arkansaw", certified 8 Jul 1806.
Territorial Papers of the US - volume: 13 page: 546

Repler, Leonard,   Louisiana-Missouri Territory   Arkansas District County,,
        Repler, Leonard,   Male
He was appointed "Capt of Infantry" in the militia for the "District of Arkansaw", certified 8 Jul 1806.
Territorial Papers of the US - volume: 13 page: 549

Repler, Leonard,   Louisiana-Missouri Territory   Arkansas District County,,
        Repler, Leonard,   Male
He was appointed one of the "Justices of the peace and common Pleas" for the "District of Arkansaw", certified 8 Jul 1806.
Territorial Papers of the US - volume: 13 page: 546

Robin, Charles,   Louisiana-Missouri Territory
        Robin, Charles, Male
Name on petition, 9 Sep 1811, to Congress from inhabitants of Arkansas (most depend on agriculture) stating that executive/legislative/judicial power is combined in one & 2/3 of their claims were rejected. They seek representative government [471-79].
Territorial Papers of the US - volume: 14 page: 472

Robine, Charles,   Louisiana-Missouri Territory
        Robine, Charles,   Male
Name on a petition, referred 11 Mar 1812, to Congress by inhabitants of Arkansas District seeking help, stating they were unaware of the deadline for filing claims. Many had received Spanish grants 10 to 25 years previously [pages 526-29].
Territorial Papers of the US - volume: 14 page: 528

Robuck, george,   Louisiana-Missouri Territory
        Robuck, george,   Male
Name on a petition, received 14 Apr 1812, to the Secretary of War from inhabitants of Arkansas District expressing concern about the hostile attitude of the Cherokees nearby. They ask for

"two or more Companies" for protection [pages 544-45].
Territorial Papers of the US - volume: 14 page: 545
Rushing, Noah,   Louisiana-Missouri Territory
        Rushing, Noah, Male
Name on a petition, referred 11 Mar 1812, to Congress by inhabitants of Arkansas District seeking help, stating they were unaware of the deadline for filing claims. Many had received Spanish grants 10 to 25 years previously [pages 526-29].
Territorial Papers of the US - volume: 14 page: 528
Rushing, Noah,   Louisiana-Missouri Territory
        Rushing, Noah, Male
Name on petition, 9 Sep 1811, to Congress from inhabitants of Arkansas (most depend on agriculture)   stating   that executive/legislative/judicial power is combined in one & 2/3 of their claims were rejected. They seek representative government [471-79].
Territorial Papers of the US - volume: 14 page: 472
Rushing, Rowland,   Louisiana-Missouri Territory
        Rushing, Rowland,   Male
Name on a petition, referred 11 Mar 1812, to Congress by inhabitants of Arkansas District seeking help, stating they were unaware of the deadline for filing claims. Many had received Spanish grants 10 to 25 years previously [pages 526-29].
Territorial Papers of the US - volume: 14 page: 528
Rushing, Rowland,   Louisiana-Missouri Territory
        Rushing, Rowland,   Male
Name on petition, 9 Sep 1811, to Congress from inhabitants of Arkansas (most depend on agriculture)   stating   that executive/legislative/judicial power is combined in one & 2/3 of their claims were rejected. They seek representative government [471-79].
Territorial Papers of the US - volume: 14 page: 472
Scull, Henry, Louisiana-Missouri Territory
        Scull, Henry,   Male

Name on a petition, referred 11 Mar 1812, to Congress by inhabitants of Arkansas District seeking help, stating they were unaware of the deadline for filing claims. Many had received Spanish grants 10 to 25 years previously [pages 526-29].
Territorial Papers of the US - volume: 14 page: 528
Scull, Hewes, Louisiana-Missouri Territory
        Scull, Hewes, Male
Name on a petition, received 14 Apr 1812, to the Secretary of War from inhabitants of Arkansas District expressing concern about the hostile attitude of the Cherokees nearby. They ask for "two or more Companies" for protection [pages 544-45].
Territorial Papers of the US - volume: 14 page: 545
Scull, Hewes, Louisiana-Missouri Territory
        Scull, Hewes, Male
Name on petition, 9 Sep 1811, to Congress from inhabitants of Arkansas (most depend on agriculture)   stating   that executive/legislative/judicial power is combined in one & 2/3 of their claims were rejected. They seek representative government [471-79].
Territorial Papers of the US - volume: 14 page: 472
Scull, James, Louisiana-Missouri   Territory
        Arkansas County
        Scull, James,   Male
He is a Township Justice "For the Settlements" on a list of civil officers dated 1 Oct 1814.
Territorial Papers of the US - volume: 14 page: 795
Scull, Jas,   Louisiana-Missouri Territory
        Scull, Jas,   Male
Name on a petition, received 14 Apr 1812, to the Secretary of War from inhabitants of Arkansas District expressing concern about the hostile attitude of the Cherokees nearby. They ask for "two or more Companies" for protection [pages 544-45].
Territorial Papers of the US - volume: 14 page: 545
Scull, Js,   Louisiana-Missouri Territory
        Scull, Js,   Male
Name on petition, 9 Sep 1811, to Congress from inhabitants of Arkansas (most depend on agriculture)   stating   that

executive/legislative/judicial power is combined in one & 2/3 of their claims were rejected. They seek representative government [471-79].
Territorial Papers of the US - volume: 14 page: 472

Seaburn, George,   Louisiana-Missouri Territory
          Seaburn, George,   Male
Name on petition, 9 Sep 1811, to Congress from inhabitants of Arkansas (most depend on agriculture) stating that executive/legislative/judicial power is combined in one & 2/3 of their claims were rejected. They seek representative government [471-79].
Territorial Papers of the US - volume: 14 page: 472

Seaburn, George,   Louisiana-Missouri Territory
          Seaburn, George,   Male
Name on a petition, referred 11 Mar 1812, to Congress by inhabitants of Arkansas District seeking help, stating they were unaware of the deadline for filing claims. Many had received Spanish grants 10 to 25 years previously [pages 526-29].
Territorial Papers of the US - volume: 14 page: 528

Silemont, Antoine,   Louisiana-Missouri Territory
          Silemont, Antoine,   Male
Name on a petition, referred 11 Mar 1812, to Congress by inhabitants of Arkansas District seeking help, stating they were unaware of the deadline for filing claims. Many had received Spanish grants 10 to 25 years previously [pages 526-29].
Territorial Papers of the US - volume: 14 page: 528

Slaughter, B F,   Louisiana-Missouri Territory
          Slaughter, B F, Male
Name on petition, 9 Sep 1811, to Congress from inhabitants of Arkansas (most depend on agriculture) stating that executive/legislative/judicial power is combined in one & 2/3 of their claims were rejected. They seek representative government [471-79].
Territorial Papers of the US - volume: 14 page: 472

Slaughtre, R F,   Louisiana-Missouri Territory
          Slaughtre, R F, Male
Name on a petition, received 14 Apr 1812, to the Secretary of War from inhabitants of Arkansas District expressing concern about the hostile attitude of the Cherokees nearby. They ask for "two or more Companies" for protection [pages 544-45].
Territorial Papers of the US - volume: 14 page: 545

Smith, Jas,   Louisiana-Missouri Territory
          Smith, Jas,   Male
Name on a petition, referred 11 Mar 1812, to Congress by inhabitants of Arkansas District seeking help, stating they were unaware of the deadline for filing claims. Many had received Spanish grants 10 to 25 years previously [pages 526-29].
Territorial Papers of the US - volume: 14 page: 528

Snyder, Philip,   Louisiana-Missouri Territory
          Snyder, Philip, Male
Name on petition, 9 Sep 1811, to Congress from inhabitants of Arkansas (most depend on agriculture) stating that executive/legislative/judicial power is combined in one & 2/3 of their claims were rejected. They seek representative government [471-79].
Territorial Papers of the US - volume: 14 page: 472

Snyder, Philip,   Louisiana-Missouri Territory
          Snyder, Philip, Male
Name on a petition, received 14 Apr 1812, to the Secretary of War from inhabitants of Arkansas District expressing concern about the hostile attitude of the Cherokees nearby. They ask for "two or more Companies" for protection [pages 544-45].
Territorial Papers of the US - volume: 14 page: 545

Snyder, Philip,   Louisiana-Missouri Territory
          Snyder, Philip, Male
Name on a petition, referred 11 Mar 1812, to Congress by inhabitants of Arkansas District seeking help, stating they were unaware of the deadline for filing claims. Many had received

Spanish grants 10 to 25 years previously [pages 526-29].
Territorial Papers of the US - volume: 14 page: 528
Souret, pier,   Louisiana-Missouri Territory
Souret, pier,   Male
He signed his name with an "x".
Name on petition, 9 Sep 1811, to Congress from inhabitants of Arkansas (most depend on agriculture) stating that executive/legislative/judicial power is combined in one & 2/3 of their claims were rejected. They seek representative government [471-79].
Territorial Papers of the US - volume: 14 page: 472
Ste greger, ,   Louisiana-Missouri Territory
Ste greger, ,   Male
He signed his name with an "x".
Name on a petition, referred 11 Mar 1812, to Congress by inhabitants of Arkansas District seeking help, stating they were unaware of the deadline for filing claims. Many had received Spanish grants 10 to 25 years previously [pages 526-29].
Territorial Papers of the US - volume: 14 page: 528
Stillwell, Harold,   Louisiana-Missouri Territory
Stillwell, Harold,   Male
Name on a petition, received 14 Apr 1812, to the Secretary of War from inhabitants of Arkansas District expressing concern about the hostile attitude of the Cherokees nearby. They ask for "two or more Companies" for protection [pages 544-45].
Territorial Papers of the US - volume: 14 page: 545
Stillwell, Joseph,   Louisiana-Missouri Territory   Arkansas County
Stillwell, Joseph,   Male
He is a Judge for Arkansas County on a list of civil officers dated 1 Oct 1814.
Territorial Papers of the US - volume: 14 page: 795
Stillwell, Joseph,   Louisiana-Missouri Territory   Arkansas District County,,
Stillwell, Joseph,   Male
He was appointed "Judge of Probate" for the "District of Arkansaw", certified 8 Jul 1806.

Territorial Papers of the US - volume: 13 page: 546
Stillwell, Joseph,   Louisiana-Missouri Territory
Stillwell, Joseph,   Male
Name on a petition, received 14 Apr 1812, to the Secretary of War from inhabitants of Arkansas District expressing concern about the hostile attitude of the Cherokees nearby. They ask for "two or more Companies" for protection [pages 544-45].
Territorial Papers of the US - volume: 14 page: 545
Strong, John,   Louisiana-Missouri Territory
Strong, John,   Male
Name on a petition, referred 11 Mar 1812, to Congress by inhabitants of Arkansas District seeking help, stating they were unaware of the deadline for filing claims. Many had received Spanish grants 10 to 25 years previously [pages 526-29].
Territorial Papers of the US - volume: 14 page: 528
Strong, John,   Louisiana-Missouri Territory
Strong, John,   Male
Name on petition, 9 Sep 1811, to Congress from inhabitants of Arkansas (most depend on agriculture) stating that executive/legislative/judicial power is combined in one & 2/3 of their claims were rejected. They seek representative government [471-79].
Territorial Papers of the US - volume: 14 page: 472
Surville, Auguste,   Louisiana-Missouri Territory
Surville, Auguste,   Male
Name on a petition, received 14 Apr 1812, to the Secretary of War from inhabitants of Arkansas District expressing concern about the hostile attitude of the Cherokees nearby. They ask for "two or more Companies" for protection [pages 544-45].
Territorial Papers of the US - volume: 14 page: 545
Tandron, Alexi,   Louisiana-Missouri Territory
Tandron, Alexi,   Male
He signed his name with an "x".
Name on a petition, referred 11 Mar 1812, to Congress by inhabitants of Arkansas District

seeking help, stating they were unaware of the deadline for filing claims. Many had received Spanish grants 10 to 25 years previously [pages 526-29].
Territorial Papers of the US - volume: 14 page: 528

Taylor, Peter, Louisiana-Missouri Territory
Taylor, Peter, Male
Name on a petition, referred 11 Mar 1812, to Congress by inhabitants of Arkansas District seeking help, stating they were unaware of the deadline for filing claims. Many had received Spanish grants 10 to 25 years previously [pages 526-29].
Territorial Papers of the US - volume: 14 page: 528

Taylor, Peter, Louisiana-Missouri Territory
Taylor, Peter, Male
Name on petition, 9 Sep 1811, to Congress from inhabitants of Arkansas (most depend on agriculture) stating that executive/legislative/judicial power is combined in one & 2/3 of their claims were rejected. They seek representative government [471-79].
Territorial Papers of the US - volume: 14 page: 472

Treat, John B., Louisiana-Missouri Territory Arkansas District County,,
Treat, John B., Male
He was appointed one of the "Justices of the peace and common Pleas" for the "District of Arkansaw", certified 8 Jul 1806.
Territorial Papers of the US - volume: 13 page: 546

Treat, Saml, Louisiana-Missouri Territory New Madrid County
Treat, Saml, Male
On 1 Apr 1813, he was made a Township Justice for the "Village of Arkansas & adjt Settlements".
Territorial Papers of the US - volume: 14 page: 650

Treat, Saml, Louisiana-Missouri Territory
Treat, Saml, Male
Name on a petition, received 14 Apr 1812, to the Secretary of War from inhabitants of Arkansas District expressing concern about the hostile attitude of the Cherokees nearby. They ask for "two or more Companies" for protection [pages 544-45].

Territorial Papers of the US - volume: 14 page: 545

Treat, Saml, Louisiana-Missouri Territory
Treat, Saml, Male
Name on a petition, referred 11 Mar 1812, to Congress by inhabitants of Arkansas District seeking help, stating they were unaware of the deadline for filing claims. Many had received Spanish grants 10 to 25 years previously [pages 526-29].
Territorial Papers of the US - volume: 14 page: 528

Treat, Samuel, Louisiana-Missouri Territory
Treat, Samuel, Male
Name on petition, 9 Sep 1811, to Congress from inhabitants of Arkansas (most depend on agriculture) stating that executive/legislative/judicial power is combined in one & 2/3 of their claims were rejected. They seek representative government [471-79].
Territorial Papers of the US - volume: 14 page: 472

Trudo, Francis, Louisiana-Missouri Territory
Trudo, Francis, Male
He signed his name with an "x".
Name on a petition, received 14 Apr 1812, to the Secretary of War from inhabitants of Arkansas District expressing concern about the hostile attitude of the Cherokees nearby. They ask for "two or more Companies" for protection [pages 544-45].
Territorial Papers of the US - volume: 14 page: 545

Valier, Francois, Louisiana-Missouri Territory Arkansas District County,,
Valier, Francois, Male
He was appointed "Capt of Cavalry" in the militia for the "District of Arkansaw", certified 8 Jul 1806.
Territorial Papers of the US - volume: 13 page: 549

Vallier, Francois, Louisiana-Missouri Territory Arkansas District County,,
Vallier, Francois, Male
He was appointed one of the "Justices of the peace and common Pleas" for the "District of Arkansaw", certified 8 Jul 1806.
Territorial Papers of the US - volume: 13 page: 546

Vasseaur, Victor,   Louisiana-Missouri Territory
            Vasseaur, Victor,   Male
Name on a petition, received 14 Apr 1812, to the Secretary of War from inhabitants of Arkansas District expressing concern about the hostile attitude of the Cherokees nearby. They ask for "two or more Companies" for protection [pages 544-45].
Territorial Papers of the US - volume: 14 page: 545

Vasseur, Etiene,   Louisiana-Missouri Territory
            Vasseur, Etiene,   Male
Name on petition, 9 Sep 1811, to Congress from inhabitants of Arkansas (most depend on agriculture)   stating   that executive/legislative/judicial power is combined in one & 2/3 of their claims were rejected. They seek representative government [471-79].
Territorial Papers of the US - volume: 14 page: 472

Vasseur, Etiene,   Louisiana-Missouri Territory
            Vasseur, Etiene,   Male
Name on a petition, referred 11 Mar 1812, to Congress by inhabitants of Arkansas District seeking help, stating they were unaware of the deadline for filing claims. Many had received Spanish grants 10 to 25 years previously [pages 526-29].
Territorial Papers of the US - volume: 14 page: 528

Vaugine, Etienne,   Louisiana-Missouri Territory
            Vaugine, Etienne,   Male
Name on a petition, referred 11 Mar 1812, to Congress by inhabitants of Arkansas District seeking help, stating they were unaware of the deadline for filing claims. Many had received Spanish grants 10 to 25 years previously [pages 526-29].
Territorial Papers of the US - volume: 14 page: 528

Vaugine, Francois,   Louisiana-Missouri Territory
            Vaugine, Francois,   Male
Name on a petition, received 14 Apr 1812, to the Secretary of War from inhabitants of Arkansas District expressing concern about the hostile attitude of the Cherokees nearby. They ask for "two or more Companies" for protection [pages 544-45].
Territorial Papers of the US - volume: 14 page: 545

Vaugine, Francois,   Louisiana-Missouri Territory   Arkansas District County,,
            Vaugine, Francois,   Male
He was appointed Major in the militia for the "District of Arkansaw", certified 8 Jul 1806.
Territorial Papers of the US - volume: 13 page: 549

Vaugine, Francois,   Louisiana-Missouri Territory
            Vaugine, Francois,   Male
Name on a petition, referred 11 Mar 1812, to Congress by inhabitants of Arkansas District seeking help, stating they were unaware of the deadline for filing claims. Many had received Spanish grants 10 to 25 years previously [pages 526-29].
Territorial Papers of the US - volume: 14 page: 528

Vaugine, francois,   Louisiana-Missouri Territory
            Vaugine, francois,   Male
Name on petition, 9 Sep 1811, to Congress from inhabitants of Arkansas (most depend on agriculture)   stating   that executive/legislative/judicial power is combined in one & 2/3 of their claims were rejected. They seek representative government [471-79].
Territorial Papers of the US - volume: 14 page: 472

Vaugine, Francois,   Louisiana-Missouri Territory   Arkansas District County,,
            Vaugine, Francois,   Male
He was appointed one of the "Justices of the peace and common Pleas" for the "District of Arkansaw", certified 8 Jul 1806.
Territorial Papers of the US - volume: 13 page: 546

Villere, Louis, Louisiana-Missouri Territory
            Villere, Louis, Male
Name on a petition, received 14 Apr 1812, to the Secretary of War from inhabitants of Arkansas District expressing concern about the hostile attitude of the Cherokees nearby. They ask for "two or more Companies" for protection [pages 544-45].

Territorial Papers of the US - volume: 14 page: 545

Wallis, Horace, Louisiana-Missouri Territory
Wallis, Horace, Male
Name on a petition, received 14 Apr 1812, to the Secretary of War from inhabitants of Arkansas District expressing concern about the hostile attitude of the Cherokees nearby. They ask for "two or more Companies" for protection [pages 544-45].
Territorial Papers of the US - volume: 14 page: 545

Wallis, Perly, Louisiana-Missouri Territory
Wallis, Perly, Male
Name on a petition, received 14 Apr 1812, to the Secretary of War from inhabitants of Arkansas District expressing concern about the hostile attitude of the Cherokees nearby. They ask for "two or more Companies" for protection [pages 544-45].
Territorial Papers of the US - volume: 14 page: 545

Wallis, Perly, Louisiana-Missouri Territory
Wallis, Perly, Male
Name on petition, 9 Sep 1811, to Congress from inhabitants of Arkansas (most depend on agriculture) stating that executive/legislative/judicial power is combined in one & 2/3 of their claims were rejected. They seek representative government [471-79].
Territorial Papers of the US - volume: 14 page: 472

Ware, Wm, Louisiana-Missouri Territory
Ware, Wm, Male
Name on a petition, referred 11 Mar 1812, to Congress by inhabitants of Arkansas District seeking help, stating they were unaware of the deadline for filing claims. Many had received Spanish grants 10 to 25 years previously [pages 526-29].
Territorial Papers of the US - volume: 14 page: 528

Ware, Wm, Louisiana-Missouri Territory
Ware, Wm, Male
Name on petition, 9 Sep 1811, to Congress from inhabitants of Arkansas (most depend on agriculture) stating that executive/legislative/judicial power is combined in

one & 2/3 of their claims were rejected. They seek representative government [471-79].
Territorial Papers of the US - volume: 14 page: 472

Wilkins, John, Louisiana-Missouri Territory
Wilkins, John, Male
Name on petition, 9 Sep 1811, to Congress from inhabitants of Arkansas (most depend on agriculture) stating that executive/legislative/judicial power is combined in one & 2/3 of their claims were rejected. They seek representative government [471-79].
Territorial Papers of the US - volume: 14 page: 472

Wilkins, John, Louisiana-Missouri Territory
Wilkins, John, Male
Name on a petition, referred 11 Mar 1812, to Congress by inhabitants of Arkansas District seeking help, stating they were unaware of the deadline for filing claims. Many had received Spanish grants 10 to 25 years previously [pages 526-29].
Territorial Papers of the US - volume: 14 page: 528

Williams, Brooks, Louisiana-Missouri Territory
Williams, Brooks, Male
Name on petition, 9 Sep 1811, to Congress from inhabitants of Arkansas (most depend on agriculture) stating that executive/legislative/judicial power is combined in one & 2/3 of their claims were rejected. They seek representative government [471-79].
Territorial Papers of the US - volume: 14 page: 472

Williams, Brooks, Louisiana-Missouri Territory
Williams, Brooks, Male
Name on a petition, referred 11 Mar 1812, to Congress by inhabitants of Arkansas District seeking help, stating they were unaware of the deadline for filing claims. Many had received Spanish grants 10 to 25 years previously [pages 526-29].
Territorial Papers of the US - volume: 14 page: 528

Williams, John, Louisiana-Missouri Territory
Williams, John, Male

Name on petition, 9 Sep 1811, to Congress from inhabitants of Arkansas (most depend on agriculture) stating that executive/legislative/judicial power is combined in one & 2/3 of their claims were rejected. They seek representative government [471-79].
Territorial Papers of the US - volume: 14 page: 472

Williams, John,   Louisiana-Missouri Territory
        Williams, John,   Male
Name on a petition, referred 11 Mar 1812, to Congress by inhabitants of Arkansas District seeking help, stating they were unaware of the deadline for filing claims. Many had received Spanish grants 10 to 25 years previously [pages 526-29].
Territorial Papers of the US - volume: 14 page: 528

Williams, Thomas,   Louisiana-Missouri Territory
        Williams, Thomas,   Male
Name on petition, 9 Sep 1811, to Congress from inhabitants of Arkansas (most depend on agriculture) stating that executive/legislative/judicial power is combined in one & 2/3 of their claims were rejected. They seek representative government [471-79].
Territorial Papers of the US - volume: 14 page: 472

Williams, Thomas,   Louisiana-Missouri Territory
        Williams, Thomas,   Male
Name on a petition, referred 11 Mar 1812, to Congress by inhabitants of Arkansas District seeking help, stating they were unaware of the deadline for filing claims. Many had received Spanish grants 10 to 25 years previously [pages 526-29].
Territorial Papers of the US - volume: 14 page: 528

Winter, W H, Louisiana-Missouri Territory
        Winter, W H,   Male
Name on a petition, received 14 Apr 1812, to the Secretary of War from inhabitants of Arkansas District expressing concern about the hostile attitude of the Cherokees nearby. They ask for "two or more Companies" for protection [pages 544-45].

Territorial Papers of the US - volume: 14 page: 545

Winter, William,   Louisiana-Missouri Territory   Arkansas District County,,
        Winter, William,   Male
He was appointed "Prothonotary and Clerk of Sessions" for the "District of Arkansaw", certified 8 Jul 1806.
Territorial Papers of the US - volume: 13 page: 546

Winter, William,   Louisiana-Missouri Territory
        Winter, William,   Male
Name on a petition, referred 11 Mar 1812, to Congress by inhabitants of Arkansas District seeking help, stating they were unaware of the deadline for filing claims. Many had received Spanish grants 10 to 25 years previously [pages 526-29].
Territorial Papers of the US - volume: 14 page: 528

Wolf, Anthony,   Louisiana-Missouri Territory
        Wolf, Anthony,   Male
Name on petition, 9 Sep 1811, to Congress from inhabitants of Arkansas (most depend on agriculture) stating that executive/legislative/judicial power is combined in one & 2/3 of their claims were rejected. They seek representative government [471-79].
Territorial Papers of the US - volume: 14 page: 472

Wolf, Anthy, Louisiana-Missouri   Territory   Arkansas District County,,
        Wolf, Anthy,   Male
He was appointed "Lt of Infantry" in the militia for the "District of Arkansaw", certified 8 Jul 1806.
Territorial Papers of the US - volume: 13 page: 549

Young, Isham, Louisiana-Missouri Territory
        Young, Isham, Male
Name on petition, 9 Sep 1811, to Congress from inhabitants of Arkansas (most depend on agriculture) stating that executive/legislative/judicial power is combined in one & 2/3 of their claims were rejected. They seek representative government [471-79].
Territorial Papers of the US - volume: 14 page: 472

Young, Isham, Louisiana-Missouri Territory

Young, Isham, Male

Name on a petition, referred 11 Mar 1812, to Congress by inhabitants of Arkansas District seeking help, stating they were unaware of the deadline for filing claims. Many had received Spanish grants 10 to 25 years previously [pages 526-29].

Territorial Papers of the US - volume: 14 page: 528

STEMMONS PUBLISHING, 1078 Shields Lane, South Jordan, Utah 84095, 801-254-2152 (Call between 9:00 a.m. and 5:00 p.m. Monday through Friday. If no one answers, please leave a message.), stemmonspublishing@gmail.com

The importance of census records and other population lists cannot be overstated in terms of the help they are in locating people in a specific area. This allows one to examine other records in that area. This is one of our main goals and why we do business. What we are trying to accomplish is a work in progress. We hope to improve as we go along. Thank you for your patience.

Petitions are an important example of these population lists.

Thank you for the opportunity to serve you.

Sincerely,
John Stemmons

A COMPLETE LIST OF OUR GENEALOGY BOOKS

AL-01 **ALABAMA 1800 PETITIONERS [-1804]**© Compiled by John D Stemmons, 2021. This book compiled from *Territorial Papers of the United States* contains 253 entries for a very early period in Alabama's history. It may contain some biographical details and clues to prior residence. It can help substitute for the missing federal census. For information on how to obtain this book search by the title or "Books by John Stemmons" at Amazon.com. This comes automatically with a paperback binding. It includes but is not limited to petitions regarding:
- Seeking new territory due to the rapid migration from Georgia, etc.
- Petition seeking confirmation of land grants obtained from other governments.

36 Pages $7.20

AL-02 **ALABAMA 1810 PETITIONERS, ETC., [1805-1814]**© Compiled by John D Stemmons, 2021. This book compiled from *Territorial Papers of the United States* contains 1687 entries for a very early period in Alabama's history. It includes a census of Madison County, taken Jan 1809. It may contain some biographical details and clues to prior residence. It can help substitute for the missing federal census. For information on how to obtain this book search by the title or "Books by John Stemmons" at Amazon.com. This comes automatically with a paperback binding. It includes but is not limited to petitions regarding:
- Issues relating to land.
- Petition of inhabitants east of Pearl River seeking to form a new territory.
- 1809 census of Madison County.
- Inhabitants of Tombigbee seeking for their purchases from the Spanish to be duty free at "Fort Stoddart".

176 Pages $35.20

AL-03 **ALABAMA 1820 PETITIONERS, ETC., [1815-1824]**© Compiled by John D Stemmons, 2021. This book compiled from

Territorial Papers of the United States contains 3913 entries for a fast-growing period in Alabama's history. It may contain some biographical details and clues to prior residence. It can help substitute for the missing federal census. For information on how to obtain this book search by the title or "Books by John Stemmons" at Amazon.com. This comes automatically with a paperback binding. It includes but is not limited to petitions regarding:
- Merchants and traders of St. Stephens seeking to establish that town as a port of delivery.
- Inhabitants of eastern part of MS territory, who lost much income/property in the wars with England & Indians.
- Inhabitants of Alabama Territory opposing the "settlements on the western side of the Mobile & Tombigby rivers" being made part of Mississippi.
- List of Letters, 9 Jan 1819, remaining in Huntsville Post Office.
- Issues about military and local officers.
- Memorial, ref. 20 Jan 1817, to Congress from inhabitants of Mobile complaining that Ft Charlotte is indefensible.

407 Pages $81.40

AR-01 **ARKANSAS PETITIONERS, ETC. 1800, 1810 [1795-1814]**© Compiled by John D Stemmons, 2021. This book compiled from *Territorial Papers of the United States* contains 261 entries and is a partial replacement for the missing federal censuses of 1800 and 1810. As a result, it is a very helpful resource in establishing residence of people in Arkansas during that early formative period in the state's history. These people include some of earliest you will find that established the foundation of what was to become the great state that Arkansas now is. This also makes it possible to determine what other records might be available for further research. Some additional biographical details may be included, and possible relationships with others may be revealed. For information on how to obtain this book search by the title or "Books by John Stemmons" at Amazon.com.

This comes automatically with a paperback binding. It includes but is not limited to petitions regarding:
- Issues relating to land.
- Inhabitants of Arkansas District expressing concern about the hostile attitude of the Cherokees nearby.
- Issues about military and local officers.

43 Pages $8.60

AR-02 ARKANSAS PETITIONERS, ETC. 1820 [1815-1824]© Compiled by John D Stemmons, 2021. This book compiled from *Territorial Papers of the United States* contains 1936 entries and is a partial replacement for the missing federal census of 1820. As a result, it is a very helpful resource in establishing residence of people in Arkansas during that fast-growing territorial period prior to becoming a state. Unfortunately, the 1820 census is not available to help track these people. That is why this new book can help. It is even better in some respects than the census because it helps us understand some of the challenges they faced. It also makes possible the determination of other records that might be available for further research. Some additional biographical details may be included, and possible relationships with others may be revealed. Even the names of some Native Americans are included as well as a few potential residents of Oklahoma. For information on how to obtain this book search by the title or "Books by John Stemmons" at Amazon.com. This comes automatically with a paperback binding. It includes but is not limited to petitions regarding:
- Issues relating to land.
- Issues relating to Native Americans.
- Citizens of Arkansas County describing the good location of the Town of Arkansas.
- Appointments about military and local officers, etc.
- Inhabitants of Arkansas and Phillips Counties seeking a mail route from the Town of Arkansas to the "Post of Ouachita in Louisianna."
- Abstract of Grand and Petit Jurors, Oct term, 1824 listing compensation for their attendance at a Superior Court held at Little Rock.

216 Pages $43.20

1001-GEORGIA PETITIONS 1778-1784© Compiled by John D Stemmons, 2004. This book contains 256 entries for a very early period in Georgia's history. For information on how to obtain this book search by the title or "Books by John Stemmons" at Amazon.com. This comes automatically with a paperback binding. It includes but is not limited to petitions regarding:
- A desire for a new district.
- A request for local courts.
- Issues about military and local officers.
- Request for protection against enemies.
- A request for pardon, amnesty, etc.
- Description of hardship.

44 pages $8.80

1002-GEORGIA PETITIONS 1785-1794© Compiled by John D Stemmons, 2004. Contains 3720 entries which includes about 25% of the heads of household in Georgia at that time. As such this publication is an excellent substitute for the missing Georgia 1790 federal census. It even includes many names for Burke and Washington Counties which suffered severe record loss in the early years. For information on how to obtain this book search by the title or "Books by John Stemmons" at Amazon.com. This comes automatically with a paperback binding. It includes but is not limited to petitions regarding:
- Issues regarding local agencies, boundary changes, etc.
- Issues regarding religion and churches.
- Issues about military and local officers.
- Asking for measures to control slaves.
- Recommendation for a business opportunity.

- Seeking resolution of land problems, land fraud, etc.
- Asking for increased tobacco inspection fees.
- Request for protection against Indians.
- Issues about crimes, pardon, amnesty, etc.
- Description of hardship.

367 pages $73.40

IL-01 ILLINOIS PETITIONS, ETC., 1760-1810 [1755-1814]© Compiled by John D Stemmons, 2021, this book contains 3680 names from *The Territorial Papers of the U.S.* This covers a period of time even before the federal census of 1790. And while no federal censuses exists for Illinois from 1790-1810, these records nicely substitute for those missing documents. It should be noted that 1004-**A PARTIAL CENSUS FOR INDIANA TERRITORY 1810** includes most if not all the names for 1810. A study to determine that they were the same was inconclusive and so, just in the outside chance there might be some that were not the same, it was felt that they should be included. The convenience of having them together outweighs their exclusion. These records include an incredible amount of information about these early people. One can see the change from a mostly French culture to that of English. The transition was not always peaceful. Included are census records, lists of inhabitants, and much more. While the federal censuses are missing that would help track these people, these records are even better in some respects than the census because it helps us understand some of the challenges they faced. That is why this new book can help. Some additional biographical details may be included, plus possible relationships with other family members. For information on how to obtain this book search by the title or "Books by John Stemmons" at Amazon.com. This comes automatically with a paperback binding. It includes but is not limited to petitions regarding:
- Issues relating to land.
- Issues relating to Native Americans.
- List of inhabitants at Kaskaskias before 1783.
- Appointments about military and local officers, etc.
- Lands claimed and possessed by inhabitants of the District of Cahokia on or before 1783 that still existed after 29 May 1790.
- Applications for lands in the District of Cahokia by persons claiming as settlers under the state of Virginia, if the settlements were made on or before 1783 that still existed after 29 May 1790.
- List of families at the Prairie du Pont, undated, but enclosed in St. Clair's report 10 Feb 1791.

349 Pages $69.80

IN-01 THE TERRITORY NORTHWEST OF THE RIVER OHIO, PETITIONERS, ETC., 1790-1800 [1785-1804] (Present day Indiana)© Compiled by John D Stemmons, 2021. This book was compiled from *Territorial Papers of the United States.* 1790 contains 242 names found on petitions, etc., including a census of heads of household for Vincennes. 1800 only includes 76 names and so is not as valuable as 1790. The population of Indiana would have increased significantly between 1790 and 1800. This is still a very early time prior to Indiana becoming a state. Unfortunately, there is no 1790 or 1800 census existing to help track these people. Therefore, we must do what we can with what is available. That is why this new book is so helpful. It is even better in some respects than the census because it helps us understand some of the challenges they faced. It also makes possible the determination of other records that might be available for further research such as land grants. Even the names of some Native Americans are listed. Some additional biographical details may be included, plus possible relationships with other family members. For information on how to obtain this book search by the title or "Books by John Stemmons" at Amazon.com. This comes automatically with a paperback binding. It includes but is not limited to petitions regarding:
- Issues relating to land.
- Heads of families settled at Post Vincennes on or before

1783 and residents at this time [13 Jul 1790] who are
entitled to donation lands.
- Issues relating to Native Americans.
- Inhabitants of Vincennes who migrated to Vincennes
  around 1786 and received land, but never obtained a deed.
- Appointments about military and local officers, etc.

38 Pages $7.60

1003-INDIANA ELECTION RETURNS 1809, 1812© Compiled by
John D and E. Diane Stemmons, 2004. This compilation of 3576
entries includes the names found in the territorial election returns
which documents are in the Indiana Historical Society. Also included
is a poll book of an election for Dearborn County in 1809 as found in
Territorial Papers of the United States. All entries in this book are
also found in *A Partial Census for Indiana Territory 1810*. The book
Indiana Election Returns, 1809, 1812 was compiled for just the
election returns simply because they are one entire record source and
may have some value in that. For information on how to obtain this
book search by the title or "Books by John Stemmons" at
Amazon.com. This comes automatically with a paperback binding.

285 pages $57.00

1004-A PARTIAL CENSUS FOR INDIANA TERRITORY 1810©
Compiled by John D and E. Diane Stemmons, 2021. With 8602
entries this book includes name lists found in *Territorial Papers of the
United States* for Indiana Territory during the period 1805 through
1814. It also provides the names in *Indiana Election Returns 1809,
1812* listed above. Since there were approximately 4300 heads of
households in the territory in 1810, *A Partial Census for Indiana
Territory 1810* probably lists virtually every head of household in
Indiana Territory for the time period. It makes an excellent substitute
for the missing federal census for 1810. In addition, it includes names
of people living in what is now Illinois, but which was part of Indiana
Territory before 1809. Therefore, *A Partial Census for Indiana
Territory 1810* is also a partial census of Illinois in the years between
1805 to 1809. For information on how to obtain this book search by
the title or "Books by John Stemmons" at Amazon.com. This comes
automatically with a paperback binding. It includes but is not limited
to petitions regarding:
- Issues relating to land.
- Heads of families settled at Post Vincennes on or before
  1783 and residents at this time [13 Jul 1790] who are
  entitled to donation lands.
- Issues relating to Native Americans.
- Inhabitants of Vincennes who migrated to Vincennes
  around 1786 and received land, but never obtained a deed.
- Appointments about military and local officers, etc.

574 pages $114.80

KY-01 KENTUCKY 1800, BARREN COUNTY TAX BOOK©
Compiled by John D Stemmons, 2021. It contains 494 names from the
Barren County tax list and 1 from *The Territorial Papers of the U.S.*
Even though the 1800 census is missing this list it provides an
amazing amount of information that substitutes nicely for that missing
census, including white and black males aged 16-21 and those 21 and
over. This is the kind of information one would expect to find on the
census for that period. This list includes all taxable heads of
household. Some additional biographical details may be included, plus
possible relationships with other family members. The names of the
blacks may be found in court, land, and probate records. For
information on how to obtain this book search by the title or "Books
by John Stemmons" at Amazon.com. This comes automatically with a
paperback binding.

65 Pages $13.00

**LA-01 ARKANSAS PETITIONS 1800 [1795-1804] and
ORLEANS TERRITORY (NOW LOUISIANA) PETITIONS,
ETC., 1800 [1795-1804]©** Compiled by John D Stemmons, 2021.

This book was compiled from *Territorial Papers of the United States*
and contains 495 names for Louisiana and 3 from Arkansas. Since no
federal census exists for Arkansas and Louisiana for 1800, these
records nicely substitute for those missing documents. These records
include an incredible amount of information about these early people.
While the federal censuses are missing that would help track these
people, these records are even better in some respects than the census
because it helps us understand some of the challenges they faced. That
is why this new book can help. Some additional biographical details
may be included, plus possible relationships with other family
members. For information on how to obtain this book search by the
title or "Books by John Stemmons" at Amazon.com. This comes
automatically with a paperback binding. It includes but is not limited
to petitions regarding:
- Inhabitants of Pointe Coupee to Gov. Claiborne, requesting
  military aid because of fears of a slave revolt.
- Characterization of New Orleans residents, 1 July 1804.
- Address from the free people of color Jan. 1804,
  volunteering for military service.
- Memorial to Congress from merchants of New Orleans, 9
  Jan 1804, offering allegiance to the US.
- Appointments about military and local officers, etc.

47 Pages $9.40

**MO-01 MISSOURI PETITIONERS, ETC., 1780-1820 [1775-
1824]©** Compiled by John D Stemmons, 2021. This book was
compiled from *Territorial Papers of the United States* and contains 1
name for 1780, 12 names for 1790, 19 names for 1800, 5057 names
for 1810, and 1509 names for 1820. The later lists begin to approach
the number needed to include most heads of household, and nicely
substitute for missing or no censuses. These records include an
incredible amount of information about these early people. While
censuses help track people, the records this book includes are even
better in some respects than the census because it helps us understand
some of their personal feelings and challenges, they faced. Some
additional biographical details may be included, plus possible
relationships with other family members. For information on how to
obtain this book search by the title or "Books by John Stemmons" at
Amazon.com. This comes automatically with a paperback binding. It
includes but is not limited to petitions, etc., regarding:
- Resolution recommending distinction between Americans
  and Frenchmen should be done away.
- Letter from U.S. President to Chief White Hairs and the
  warriors of the Osages, informing them of the Lewis and
  Clark expedition, and promising them a resident agent.
- Many petitions, etc., expressing their support and
  confidence in Governor Wilkinson. He was involved in
  scandals and controversies.
- Memorial recommending replacements for Governor
  Wilkinson.
- Petition expressing concern about changing the form of
  territorial government before they are adequately prepared.
- Memorial concerning the large number of their Spanish
  land claims that are being rejected.
- Lists of civil and military officers.
- Petition seeking a grant of a township of land for the
  support of the school as had been done in other areas.
- Petition seeking pre-emption rights for the services given
  in defending the frontier in Boon's Lick Settlement around
  1815.
- Petitions relating to the New Madrid & Little Prairie
  earthquake.
- Petitions asking for new post offices and routes, etc.

552 pages $110.40

MI-01 MICHIGAN PETITIONS, ETC. 1790-1810 [1785-1814]©
Compiled by John D Stemmons, 2021. This book was compiled from
Territorial Papers of the United States. It contains 1 name for 1790,

794 names for 1800, and 1335 names for 1810. Clearly, that is not enough for 1790, but the others begin to approach the number needed. Especially is this so for 1810 because we are fortunate enough to have much of what appears to be the federal 1810 census. Since no federal census exists for 1800, these records nicely substitute for those missing documents. These records include an incredible amount of information about these early people. While censuses help track people, the records this book includes are even better in some respects than the census because it helps us understand some of their personal feelings and challenges, they faced. Some additional biographical details may be included, plus possible relationships with other family members. For information on how to obtain this book search by the title or "Books by John Stemmons" at Amazon.com. This comes automatically with a paperback binding. It includes but is not limited to petitions regarding:

- Inhabitants of Detroit seeking new territory because of distance to travel to the headquarters of Indiana Territory.
- Appointments about military and local officers, etc.
- Inhabitants of Wayne County seeking clarification of the status of their land.
- 1810 Census of the District of Detroit.
- Inhabitants of Michigan Ter. seeking time to file claims to their land.
- List, 23 Jul 1812, of patents received from the General Land Office for private claims in the District of Detroit.
- Petition from inhabitants of Michigan Territory asking that the new territorial code be printed also in French.
- Petition to Thomas Jefferson, from inhabitants of Michigan Territory complaining of Governor William Hull and Supreme Court Chief Justice Augustus B. Woodward.

222 Pages $44.40

MS-01 MISSISSIPPI TERRITORIAL PETITIONERS, ETC. 1800 [1795-1804]© Compiled by John D Stemmons, 2021. This book was compiled from *Territorial Papers of the United States and* contains 2566 names found on petitions, etc., from Mississippi Territory for this time period. This was during a fast-growing era prior to Mississippi becoming a state. Unfortunately, there is no 1800 census existing to help track these people. That is why this new book can help. It is even better in some respects than the census because it helps us understand some of the challenges they faced. It also makes possible the determination of other records that might be available for further research such as Spanish land grants. Some additional biographical details may be included, plus possible relationships with other family members. For information on how to obtain this book search by the title or "Books by John Stemmons" at Amazon.com. This comes automatically with a paperback binding. It includes but is not limited to petitions regarding:

- Citizens of territory asking land office to be in the area, settlers have pre-emption right, & suffrage be for males of age and US citizens & residents of territory for 6 months.
- Memorial by citizens of the territory, who obtained land before the area became part of the US.
- Testimonials, ca 1802, by individuals regarding the service of John Steele, secretary of the territory.
- Memorial by citizens of the territory seeking that "moderate grants [be] made to actual settlers on unappropriated lands,"
- Merchants of Natchez, complaining of the extra duties they must pay for merchandise shipped from the US.

209 Pages $41.80

MS-02 MISSISSIPPI TERRITORIAL PETITIONS, ETC. 1810 [1805-1814] and WEST FLORIDA 1820 PETITIONERS [1815-1824]© Compiled by John D Stemmons, 2021. This book was compiled from *Territorial Papers of the United States* and contains 1061 names found on petitions, etc., from Mississippi Territory for the period 1810 [1805-1814]. It also includes a list of 76 names on a petition to Congress, 11 Dec 1816, by inhabitants of Jackson County, Mississippi Territory, many of whom settled on land in West Florida while under Spanish control and now seek for their grant to be confirmed by the US. It is being included with Mississippi Territory because it is basically the same time period and place of residence. This was during a fast-growing time prior to Mississippi and Florida becoming states. Unfortunately, there is no 1810 or 1820 census existing to help track these people. That is why this new book can help. It is even better in some respects than the census because it helps us understand some of the challenges they faced. It also makes possible the determination of other records that might be available for further research. Some additional biographical details may be included, and possible relationships with others may be revealed. For information on how to obtain this book search by the title or "Books by John Stemmons" at Amazon.com. This comes automatically with a paperback binding. It includes but is not limited to petitions regarding:

- Inhabitants of the territory seeking adjustment of land claims obtained from the British Government.
- Inhabitants of the territory seek for a road to be built that follows the Pearl River which would shorten the route from Nashville to New Orleans.
- Inhabitants of Amite and Wilkinson Counties seek establishment of a post office.
- Memorial by citizens of the territory (Americans by birth?) seeking a postponement of statehood for the territory.
- Inhabitants of Jackson Co., Mississippi Territory, many of whom settled on land in West Florida while under Spanish control seek for their grant to be confirmed by the US.

108 Pages $21.60

NJ-01-NEW JERSEY PETITIONS 1740, 1745 THROUGH 1754© Compiled by John D Stemmons, 2021. It contains 740 entries for a period of time in New Jersey when records are sparse. While that may not seem like very many names, it was during the time when the population was small, and the residence of people was sometimes hard to track. In looking through these petitions, it appears that the people of this era had basically the same concerns we have. One can see the forces of democracy beginning to stir that were to result in independence from Great Britain just a short three decades away. We can obtain a hint of the personal concerns of these people and what was important to them in this exciting historical time. Even at this time of great distress and hardship life had to go on. These petitions are almost like an open window into the lives of these people. For information on how to obtain this book search by the title or "Books by John Stemmons" at Amazon.com. This comes automatically with a paperback binding. It includes but is not limited to petitions regarding:

- Issues regarding exports and imports.
- Issues regarding devaluation of currency, money supply, etc.
- Issues regarding local agencies, boundary changes, etc.
- Seeking new legislation.
- Issues about military and government officers.
- Seeking resolution of land problems, etc.
- Protesting against the great number of taverns.
- Resolution of tax issues.
- Issues about crimes, pardon, amnesty, etc.

84 pages $16.80

NJ-02-NEW JERSEY PETITIONS 1755-1764© Compiled by John D Stemmons, 2004. Contains 2389 entries from many petitions submitted because of concerns about the French and Indian War. This book is an excellent census substitute. For information on how to obtain this book search by the title or "Books by John Stemmons" at Amazon.com. This comes automatically with a paperback binding. It includes petitions regarding:

- Issues regarding local agencies, boundary changes, etc.
- Issues about roads, bridges, etc.

- Opposition to importing slaves.
- Seeking naturalization.
- Seeking new legislation.
- Issues about military and government affairs.
- Request for reimbursement from the government.
- Request for protection against enemies.
- Seeking resolution of land problems, etc.
- Protesting against dispensing of "spirituous liquors"
- Issues about crimes, pardon, amnesty, etc.
- Description of hardship.

246 pages $49.20

NJ-03-NEW JERSEY PETITIONS 1765-1774© Compiled by John D Stemmons, 2004. This book contains 806 entries. While a small percent of the population, it represents the time leading up to the Revolution. For information on how to obtain this book search by the title or "Books by John Stemmons" at Amazon.com. This comes automatically with a paperback binding. It includes but is not limited to petitions regarding:

- Issues regarding agriculture, exports and imports.
- Request for permission to beg, financial support, etc.
- Issues about religion and churches.
- Request for medical standards.
- Issues regarding devaluation of currency, money supply, etc.
- Issues regarding local agencies, boundary changes, etc.
- Issues on hunting, fishing, etc.
- Issues about roads, bridges, etc.
- Issues relating to slavery.
- Issues about military and government affairs.
- Seeking resolution of land problems, etc.
- Issues about crimes, pardon, amnesty, etc.

99 pages $19.80

NJ-04-NEW JERSEY PETITIONS 1775-1784© Compiled by John D Stemmons, 2005. This book contains 6201 entries which is about 29% of the heads of household living in New Jersey at that time (not counting duplicate names.) It represents the historic period during the Revolution. For information on how to obtain this book search by the title or "Books by John Stemmons" at Amazon.com. This comes automatically with a paperback binding. It includes but is not limited to petitions regarding:

- Issues regarding trade, exports, and imports.
- Issues regarding devaluation of currency, money supply, price controls, etc.
- Issues on religion and churches.
- Issues regarding local agencies, boundary changes or disputes, etc.
- Issues on court cases.
- Request for guardianship of children.
- Issues about roads, bridges, canals, etc.
- Issues on slavery.
- Seeking new legislation or repealing old laws.
- Issues about military and government affairs and officers.
- Issues about payment from the government.
- Issues on independence and the Revolutionary War.
- Request for protection against enemies.
- Seeking resolution of property and land problems, etc.
- Issues about crimes, pardon, amnesty, etc.
- Resolution of tax issues.

559 pages $111.80

NJ-05-NEW JERSEY PETITIONS 1785-1794 Volumes 1-2© Compiled by John D Stemmons, 2005. This book contains 10,353 entries which covers about 35% of the heads of household for that time, not counting duplicate names. For information on how to obtain this book search by the title or "Books by John Stemmons" at

Amazon.com. This comes automatically with a paperback binding. It includes but is not limited to petitions regarding:

- Economic issues regarding the devaluation of currency, public debt, etc.
- Issues on religion and churches.
- Issues regarding counties and towns, etc.
- Issues on court cases.
- Issues regarding hunting on private property, fishing, etc.
- Issues about roads, bridges, canals, ferries, etc.
- Issues relating to schools.
- Issues on slavery.
- Seeking new legislation or repealing existing laws.
- Issues about military and government affairs and officers.
- Seeking payment from the government.
- Expressing approval of the U.S. Constitution.
- Seeking resolution of property and land problems, etc.
- Issues about crimes, pardon, amnesty, etc.
- Resolution of tax issues.

Volume 1, A Through K, pages 462 $92.40
Volume 2, L Through Z, pages 470 $94.00

NJ-06 NEW JERSEY PETITIONERS, ETC., 1800 [1795-1804] Volumes 1-3© Compiled by John Stemmons, 2021. All volumes of this book contain 13,144 names. Unlike the tax ratables, these records cover the entire state for the period just after the Revolutionary War These records provide a place of residence which can lead to other records to search. For information on how to obtain this book search by the title or "Books by John Stemmons" at Amazon.com. This comes automatically with a paperback binding. It includes but is not limited to petitions regarding:

- Public buildings including poor house, taverns, banks, etc.
- Issues on religion and churches.
- Issues regarding counties and towns, etc.
- Issues on court cases.
- Concerning voting opportunities
- Issues about roads, bridges, canals, ferries, water rights, storage of gunpowder, etc.
- Issues relating to schools.
- Issues on slavery.
- Seeking new legislation or repealing existing laws.
- Issues about military and government affairs and officers.
- Seeking payment from the government.
- Seeking resolution of property and land problems, etc.
- Issues about crimes, pardon, amnesty, etc.
- Resolution of tax issues.

Volume 1, A Through E, pages 423 $84.60
Volume 2, F Through R, pages 529 $105.80
Volume 3, S Through Z, pages 358 $71.60

NJ-07 NEW JERSEY TAX RATABLES, 1770 [1765-1774] This book contains 2373 names of those who are taxable. They do include important details about the property they held and may provide clues regarding relationship, etc. For information on how to obtain this book search by the title or "Books by John Stemmons" at Amazon.com. This comes automatically with a paperback binding.

250 pages $50.00

NJ-08 NEW JERSEY TAX RATABLES, 1780 [1775-1784] This book contains 4358 names of those who are taxable. It includes important details about the property they held and may provide clues regarding relationship, etc. For information on how to obtain this book search by the title or "Books by John Stemmons" at Amazon.com. This comes automatically with a paperback binding.

440 pages $88.00

NJ-09 NEW JERSEY TAX RATABLES, 1790 [1785-1794] This book contains 2307 names of those who are taxable. Unfortunately,

Burlington and Cape May counties are not covered by this period. We are fortunate though in have the petitions that cover the same time. It is interesting to compare the two sets of records. They were not combined because that would make the books too large. The tax ratables do include important details about the property they held and may provide clues regarding relationship, etc. For information on how to obtain this book search by the title or "Books by John Stemmons" at Amazon.com. This comes automatically with a paperback binding.
268 pages $53.60

NJ-10 NEW JERSEY TAX RATABLES, 1800 [1795-1804] , Volumes 1-2 This book contains 8396 names of those who are taxable. It includes important details about the property they held and may provide clues regarding relationship, etc. For information on how to obtain this book search by the title or "Books by John Stemmons" at Amazon.com. This comes automatically with a paperback binding.
Volume 1, A Through K, pages 456 $91.20
Volume 2, L Through Z, pages 449 $89.80

NC-01 NORTH CAROLINA PETITIONERS, ETC. 1780 [1775-1784]© Compiled by John Stemmons, 2021. This book contains 4866 names and was assembled from records located at the North Carolina State Archives. This was before the federal census was taken and is a valuable resource for locating people in this early time. Included are some names from what is now, Tennessee. For information on how to obtain this book search by the title or "Books by John Stemmons" at Amazon.com. This comes automatically with a paperback binding.
- Economic issues regarding the devaluation of currency, public debt, etc.
- Issues on religion and churches.
- Issues regarding counties and towns, etc.
- Issues regarding hunting on private property, fishing, etc.
- Issues about roads, bridges, canals, ferries, etc.
- Seeking new legislation or repealing existing laws.
- Issues about military and government affairs and officers.
- Seeking resolution of property and land problems, etc.
- Issues about crimes, pardon, amnesty, etc.

568 pages $113.60

1009-ROWAN COUNTY, NORTH CAROLINA TAX LISTS 1758/1759, 1761, 1768, 1778, 1779© Compiled by John D and E. Diane Stemmons, 2004. This publication serves as a census for Rowan County for about three decades which includes two major conflicts, the French and Indian and Revolutionary wars. Thus, one may be able to track individuals that stayed in the county over a significant period of time. Sometimes sons and slaves are given plus other important information. These tax lists are listed alphabetically in three separate sections.
218 pages $43.60

OH-01 TERRITORY NW OF OHIO RIVER, PETITIONERS, ETC. 1790-1800 [1785-1804] (Now Ohio)© Compiled by John D Stemmons, 2021. It contains 217 names for 1790 and 3047 names for 1800. This book may include many heads of household at that time and serves as a substitute for missing or no censuses. It even incorporates the names of many native Americans. These records provide an incredible amount of information about these early people. While censuses help track people, the records this book contains are even better in some respects than the census because it helps us understand some of their personal information not recorded by a census. Some additional biographical details may be included, plus possible relationships with other family members. For information on how to obtain this book search by the title or "Books by John Stemmons" at Amazon.com. This comes automatically with a paperback binding. It includes but is not limited to petitions regarding:
- Petition of the French inhabitants of Gallipolis regarding their purchase of lands from the Scioto Company.
- Inhabitants on the Muskingum to Governor St. Clair.
- Petitions about land and issues with John Cleves Symmes.
- 1800, Population Schedules, Washington County. Territory Northwest of the River Ohio.
- Petition by inhabitants telling of losses in the "Late Indian war" and their inability to obtain land in Kentucky.
- Petition by inhabitants of Hamilton County seeking approval to purchase reserved land in order to build a grist mill because it has a sufficient stream of water.
- List of Gallipolis proprietors and the amount of their land purchases.

285 pages $57.00

PA-01 PENNSYLVANIA CHESTER COUNTY TAX LIST 1771© Compiled by John D Stemmons, 2021. It contains 5621 names. This record lists all taxable people in the county, and as such, is a good census substitute. It is not known what is meant by the abbreviations or "inmate". Perhaps they were incarcerated in jail or were indentured in some way. Often an occupation is listed. Occasionally there will be information about family relationships. It is helpful that this book includes the information about the taxable property. For information on how to obtain this book search by the title or "Books by John Stemmons" at Amazon.com. This comes automatically with a paperback binding.
399 pages $79.80

South Carolina

South Carolina has a remarkable series of records that makes it unique for the Colonial period. These are the "Jury Lists" compiled by the government to function as a list of names from which members of a jury could be assigned. They cover the period 1720-1783 and, according to the act in 1731, were compiled from tax lists of the preceding year [which no longer exist], listing every person who paid a tax of twenty shillings or more. Those who paid five pounds or more were listed as grand jurors. The poorer class of people would not be listed. While not a complete list of the heads of household, they represent a sizeable proportion. They serve as a census during a period of growth, migration, and war. Usually only the name is given, but sometimes an occupation or name of the father is listed, etc. Many names are on more than one list for a particular year.

1010-SOUTH CAROLINA 1720 JURY LIST© Compiled by John D and E. Diane Stemmons, 2004. This publication has 840 entries covering a time when South Carolina was only 50 years old and the population was very small with only an estimated 885 heads of household. Unfortunately, it does not list a residence other than South Carolina. For information on how to obtain this book search by the title or "Books by John Stemmons" at Amazon.com. This comes automatically with a paperback binding.
48 pages $9.60

1017-SOUTH CAROLINA 1731 JURY LIST© Compiled by John D and E. Diane Stemmons, 2005. This book contains 2160 entries. It lists the locality of every person. For information on how to obtain this book search by the title or "Books by John Stemmons" at Amazon.com. This comes automatically with a paperback binding.
110 pages $22.00

1011-SOUTH CAROLINA 1740 JURY LIST© Compiled by John D and E. Diane Stemmons, 2004. This book contains 2160 entries. It lists the locality of every person. For information on how to obtain this book search by the title or "Books by John Stemmons" at Amazon.com. This comes automatically with a paperback binding.
111 pages $22.20

1012-SOUTH CAROLINA 1751 JURY LIST© Compiled by John D and E. Diane Stemmons, 2004. This book contains 2170 entries. It lists the locality of every person. For information on how to obtain this book search by the title or "Books by John Stemmons" at Amazon.com. This comes automatically with a paperback binding.

109 pages $21.80

1013-SOUTH CAROLINA 1757 JURY LIST© Compiled by John D and E. Diane Stemmons, 2004. This book contains 2624 entries. It lists the locality of every person. For information on how to obtain this book search by the title or "Books by John Stemmons" at Amazon.com. This comes automatically with a paperback binding.
135 pages $27.00

1014-SOUTH CAROLINA 1767 JURY LIST© Compiled by John D and E. Diane Stemmons, 2004. This book contains 2385 entries. It lists the locality of every person. For information on how to obtain this book search by the title or "Books by John Stemmons" at Amazon.com. This comes automatically with a paperback binding.
127 pages $25.40

SC-07 SOUTH CAROLINA 1780 [1775-1784], VOLUMES 1-2© Compiled by John D Stemmons, 2021. It contains 13,444 names. This record of jury lists consist of many people during the Colonial/Revolutionary War period and as such, is a good census substitute. Since Loyalists owned property that they paid taxes on, they may be included as well. These records provide a place of residence which can lead to other records to search. For information on how to obtain this book search by the title or "Books by John Stemmons" at Amazon.com. This comes automatically with a paperback binding.
Volume 1, 502 pages $100.40
Volume 2, 575 pages $115.00

TN-01 TENNESSEE PETITIONS, ETC., 1770-1790 [1765-1794]© Also known as Territory South of Ohio River. Compiled by John Stemmons, 2021. This book was assembled from *Territorial Papers of the United States* and contains 1 name for 1770, 12 names for 1780, and 1161 names for 1790. These people listed seem to be the more prominent persons, so, most of the less noteworthy individuals would not be listed. Still, the people listed clarify this early time before Tennessee became a state. The amount of biographical information is significant compared to the other books we have compiled from *Territorial Papers of the United States*. Many Native American names are included. For information on how to obtain this book search by the title or "Books by John Stemmons" at Amazon.com. This comes automatically with a paperback binding. It includes but is not limited to petitions regarding:
- "One of twelve men selected by the Cumberland people to govern the settlement, 1783; appointed by the Governor of North Carolina judge of the courts, Davidson County, 1783.
- Appointments about military and local officers, etc.
- Name on the "Treaty of Holston", 2 Jul 1791 between the President of the US and "Chiefs and Warriors of the Cherokee Nation of Indians."
- Memorial, 1 Aug 1791, to the President from the civil and military officers of Mero District explaining recent depredations of the Indians and seeking an "Act of Cession" from North Carolina.

95 pages $19.00

TN-02 TENNESSEE PETITIONERS, ETC. AND GRAINGER COUNTY TAX LISTS 1800 [1795-1804]© Compiled by John Stemmons, 2021. Also known as Territory South of Ohio River. This book was assembled from Grainger County Tax Lists 1800 and *Territorial Papers of the United States* and contains 182 names for the *Papers* and 247 names for the tax lists. From *Territorial Papers of the United States* the names mostly seem to be persons appointed to official or military positions or are members of the Knoxville Convention. Thus, they seem to be the more prominent persons, so, most of the less noteworthy individuals would not be listed. Still, the people listed clarify this early time before Tennessee became a state. The tax lists record the names of those who are taxable and are much more inclusive. They do include important details about the property they held. For information on how to obtain this book search by the title or "Books by John Stemmons" at Amazon.com. This comes automatically with a paperback binding. It includes but is not limited to petitions regarding:
- List, 21 Dec 1795, of members of Knoxville Convention.
- Appointments of military and local officers, etc.

49 pages $9.80

TN-03 TENNESSEE GRAINGER COUNTY TAX LISTS 1810 [1805-1814]© Compiled by John Stemmons, 2021. This book was assembled from Grainger County Tax Lists 1810 and contains 1242 names of those who are taxable. They do include important details about the property they held and may provide clues regarding relationship, etc. For information on how to obtain this book search by the title or "Books by John Stemmons" at Amazon.com. This comes automatically with a paperback binding.
146 pages $29.20

TN-04 TENNESSEE GRAINGER COUNTY TAX LISTS 1820 [1815-1824]© Compiled by John Stemmons, 2021. This book was assembled from Grainger County Tax Lists 1820 and contains 1161 names of those who are taxable. They do include important details about the property they held and may provide clues regarding relationship, etc. The lists for 1800-1820 furnish an excellent opportunity to track the population growth of the county. For information on how to obtain this book search by the title or "Books by John Stemmons" at Amazon.com. This comes automatically with a paperback binding.
131 pages $26.20

VA-01 VIRGINIA PERSONAL PROPERTY TAX LISTS, 1780 [1775-1784] (Accomack and Albemarle Counties)© Compiled by John Stemmons, 2021. This book was assembled from Accomack and Albemarle Counties Personal Property Tax Lists ca 1780 and contains 2553 names of those who are taxable. They do include important details about the property they held and may provide clues regarding relationship, etc. They even furnish the entry for, it is assumed, future president Thomas Jefferson! For information on how to obtain this book search by the title or "Books by John Stemmons" at Amazon.com. This comes automatically with a paperback binding.
252 pages $50.40

VA-02 VIRGINIA PERSONAL PROPERTY TAX LISTS, 1790 [1785-1794] (Accomack and Albemarle Counties)© Compiled by John Stemmons, 2021. This book was assembled from Accomack and Albemarle Counties Personal Property Tax Lists ca 1790 and contains 2679 names of those who are taxable, plus 3 from *Territorial Papers of the U.S.* They do include important details about the property they held and may provide clues regarding relationship, etc. They even furnish the entry for, it is assumed, future president Thomas Jefferson! Data on the age range of males is also included. For information on how to obtain this book search by the title or "Books by John Stemmons" at Amazon.com. This comes automatically with a paperback binding.
333 pages $66.60

VA-03 VIRGINIA PERSONAL PROPERTY TAX LISTS, ca 1800 [1795-1804] (Accomack and Albemarle Counties)© Compiled by John Stemmons, 2021. This book was assembled from Accomack and Albemarle Counties Personal Property Tax Lists ca 1800 and contains 3788 names of those who are taxable. They do include important details about the property they held and may provide clues regarding relationship, etc. They even furnish the entry for, it is assumed, future president Thomas Jefferson! Data on the age range of males is also included. With the lists for 1780-1800 one can track population growth in these countries. An individual showing up for the first time may indicate potential age. For information on how to

obtain this book search by the title or "Books by John Stemmons" at Amazon.com. This comes automatically with a paperback binding.
436 pages $87.20

Population estimates were obtained from U.S. Bureau of the Census, *Historical Statistics of the United States, Colonial Times to 1957,* Washington, D.C., 1960, Library of Congress Card No. A 60-9150; and United States. Bureau of the Census, *A Century of Population Growth From the First Census of the United States to the Twelfth, 1790-1900* Washington: Government Printing Office, 1909. A household size of 5.7 persons was assumed.

Good morning.

We received the gift book of "Georgia Petitions 1785-1794". Fantastic book and a great tool in researching that time period. I like the format which is easy to read and puts in one place the petitions for research. I personally have searched many of the petitions and love this new tool. The introduction and the list of petitions gives much added information to understanding the petitions for the various individuals.

I look forward to ordering more books in July after our budget is in place. Thank you for contacting our library and making us aware of your fine publications. Have a great day.

Thanks,

Irene Godwin

Ellen Payne Odom Genealogy Library

204 5th St. S.E.

P.O. Box 2828

Moultrie, GA 31768

EXAMPLES OF THE KIND OF INFORMATION CONTAINED IN OUR BOOKS

Cicotte, J. Bte.,   Michigan Territory, District of Detroit, "Cote des Poux"

Cicotte, J. Bte.,	45-Over?	Male	**Color:**	White
10-16	Male	**Color:**	White	
10-16	Male	**Color:**	White	
16-26	Male	**Color:**	White	
45-Over	Female	**Color:**	White	

1810 Census of the District of Detroit

MS/Witherell (B. F. H.) Collection, LMS, Burton Historical Collection, Detroit Public Library, Folder 2

Cicotte, Jacques,   Michigan Territory

Cicotte, Jacques,   Male

Petition, 26 Oct 1807, to Congress from inhabitants of Michigan Ter. seeking time to file claims to their land, claims on 1+ parcels be confirmed, farms on Detroit River be extended to 80 arpents, & occupancy later than 1 Jul 1796 be allowed [pp. 138-49].

Territorial Papers of the US - volume: 10 page: 146

Holeday, Jas,   Territory NW of Ohio River   Knox County, Vincennes

Holeday, Jas,   Male

Address to Colonel Josiah Harmar by American inhabitants of Post Vincennes dated 4 Aug 1787

Territorial Papers of US - volume: 2 page: 65

Holliday, Heirs of James,   Territory NW of Ohio River   Knox County, Vincennes

Holliday, Heirs of James,   Male

Petition, 7 Aug 1797, to Congress by inhabitants of Knox County, who migrated to Vincennes around 1786 and received land, but never obtained a deed.

Territorial Papers of US - volume: 2 page: 621

Lajoye, Pierre ,   Spanish North America, St. Louis

Lajoye, Pierre,   Male

"Pierre Lajoye, formerly of Prairie du Rocher on the American side of the Mississippi".

Letter, 1790, by Governor St. Clair to Manuel Perez concerning an American boy in the possession of Pierre Lajoye [pages 237-238].

"Mr. Mayet has just complained to me that a Mr. La Joye, to whom he has entrusted an American boy, whom he took from the savages, to be returned to the parents of the latter, has not returned him, but is holding the boy as a slave and refuses to return the boy to them on the pretext of some debt. I am convinced that you will not find it proper that a free child should be held as a slave for the debts of another--and will order Mr. La Joye to return him to Mayet."

Letter, 26 May 1790, from St. Louis by Manuel Perez to Governor St. Clair concerning an American boy in the possession of Pierre Lajoye [pages 237-240]:

"MY DEAR SIR: In order to take cognizance of the subject of the claim in your favor of the 20th instant concerning the child who is today in the possession of Mr. Lajoye, I had the latter appear before me and from the questions which I put to him and the reasons which he advanced to me on this subject I have found in him only a disposition to render service to the Unhappy Father who lost him and who asks for him in a letter of which the said Mr. Lajoye is the bearer.

After studying this matter carefully, I find that the above-mentioned child claimed by Mr. Mayet can leave the possession of Mr. Lajoye only to go to that of the Father now living at Natches. I think also that it is just for the said Mr. Mayet to be reimbursed for what he actually gave the savages in order to get him out of their barbarous hands; . . .

When the young man arrived at Mr. Lajoye's house, he came and notified me of it at once and that he would write to the lower part of the Colony to learn in what district the Father of the said child lived. He learned later from the letter of which he is the bearer, that he resides at Natchez; accordingly he will send him down on the first opportunity."

Territorial Papers of the US - volume: 2 page: 237

Mayfield, Geddeon, Kentucky Barren County

Mayfield, Geddeon,   Male

Acres of land: 200; Barren Co.; watercourse: Mill Creek; Entry: Geddeon Mayfield; Survey: same; Patent: 0; white males over 21: 0; white males 16-21: 0; blacks over 16: 0; total blacks: 0; horses: 0; stud horses: 0; retail stores: 0; tavern license: 0.

LEGISLATIVE PETITIONS

Petitions to the governor, legislature, etc., were a particularly important way for individuals to communicate with their government regarding issues that were very essential to them. Their influence in making changes throughout our history has contributed to making our society what it is today. They are an important link in our legislative and judicial history. In these early petitions one can trace the growing desire for democracy. In fact, they are one of the most visible manifestations of democracy in practice. It is fascinating to view the changes in the reasons for submitting petitions over time (see the lists below.)

Because petitions represent the feelings of one or more individuals, they provide a window into the soul of the petitioners that illuminates the historical landscape. Most aspects of the human condition are addressed in some form by these important documents. The names listed with the petition can be used as a census of inhabitants for a particular locality. Often it is possible to determine useful information about individual persons from these records. They can help compensate for lost or destroyed county records. Petitions are original records that contain historical background about our culture and society.

Unfortunately, petitions are among the most inaccessible and underused records because there are so many, they are often difficult and time-consuming to read, and are usually housed only in the state archives or other repository in their un-microfilmed condition.

To help resolve this problem, we have abstracted the content of many petitions and indexed the names of the petitioners. A brief context of the petition is provided with each name. Generally, we have not included those petitions with fewer than 10-12 names.

GENEALOGY AND LOCAL HISTORY BOOKS IN PDF FORMAT ON A FLASH DRIVE

705 Local and Family History books for $75-or 11 cents a book!!! All 4 volumes of Savage's Genealogical Dictionary of New England would cost you about $0.44!*

You can have in your library/home more books of this type than most libraries have. They cover nearly all aspects of human experience including law, medicine, biography, history, etc., etc.

Concerns?

1. **Question:** I am uncomfortable in letting patrons use this small drive as it may become lost.

Answer: Simply download the contents of the drive onto your computer(s) and keep the drive in a safe place. We will replace it at no charge if it becomes lost.

2. **Question:** Some of our books, including those on microfilm, that are also on your flash drive are in poor condition because of patron use through the years, especially when copies are made. Copies made from microfilm are not always the best quality. How can you help us with these problems?

Answer: Once our books are on your computers, your originals can be kept in a secured area so that no more damage will occur because of hands-on use. The images on the computer can be easily printed, usually with better quality.

3. **Question:** We are only interested in items covering the locality our patrons live in.

Answer: Many of your patrons were born outside of your area and/or have ancestry from all over the United States, etc.

4. **Question:** Are these books under copyright restrictions?

Answer: They are in the public domain and so are not copyrightable.

Approximately how many pages do the 705 books add up to?
Total cost (from Stemmons Publishing) for hard copies: $7044 (not available now)
Approximated total pages of text on the flash drive: 221,307
Approximated total images on the flash drive: 58,272

A huge genealogical library of 705 books on your computer for only $75
A dealer's discount is available of $45 for 5 or more flash drives.
Imagine 705 books… 60,417 images… 230,642 pages on a small flash drive.

You may be able to find these books on Google, Ancestry, or FamilySearch. To make a hard copy from these sources may be expensive, especially if you were to copy all 705! I may be mistaken, but I'm not sure you can print just a single page from those services. You can with my books. You also have them immediately at your fingertips without needing to go to the effort to search these other services.

The downside to these books is that many are not indexed.

No problem: just check the index provided by these other sources before using our books.

"In 2016, popular genealogy blogger Dick Eastman surmised that perhaps ninety percent of the resources you may need to fill out your family tree are not yet available on the Internet." This statement was found on the Boston Public Library website. If that is true, some of the books on our flash drive may not be found on the Internet.

You may obtain a copy of the drive by sending check, money order, or cash to John Stemmons at 1078 Shields Lane, South Jordan, Utah, 801-254-2152 (Call between 9:00 a.m. and 5:00 p.m. Monday through Friday. If no one answers, please leave a message.), stemmonspublishing@gmail.com. We have been in this business since 1975! Check BBB if you need to.

The fee for shipping and handling is $10.00 unless you send a shipping container, deliverable to you, with sufficient postage to mail to you. Please allow 4-6 weeks for delivery.

The books on the drive are in the public domain and are not copyrighted. You may make as many copies of them as you would like. Please do not place the contents of the drive, in part or in full, on the Internet except for individual pages.

We do not do credit cards and PayPal. If you are unhappy with the drive, please return it for a refund of your money.

If you would like a list of questions and answers or a list of the books, please let us know.

*How are we able to do this? Simply by reducing each page so that 2-6 pages can be placed on a single 8½ by 11 sheet of paper and still be readable. With the computer, you can enlarge it as many times as needed.

Number of books by locality:
US-99, Regional-32, AL-1, CT-31, DE-1, GA-2, IL-1, IN-1, KY-1, ME-23, MD-15, MA-91, MI-1, MN-1, MO-2, NH-20, NJ-28, NY-81, NC-9, OH-9, PA-51, RI-6, SC-26, VT-2, VA-47, WV-1; Family History-62; CN-5; EN-39; IR-10; SCOT-7=705 books!

www.ingramcontent.com/pod-product-compliance
Lightning Source LLC
Chambersburg PA
CBHW082333270726

48658CB00018B/3259